Since his death
Indian schoolchildren have been
taught to think of Gandhi as the
father of the nation. India was still
part of the British Empire when he wa
born in 1869; by the time
he died, in
1948, India was
a free country,
thanks to him.

His childhood was uneventful. He was born into a Hindu family and had a venerable old father whom he loved and respected and a pious young mother whom he adored. The young Gandhi was deeply attached to the world around him and used to climb the mango trees in the garden and bandage the 'wounded' fruit.

He may have been a model child, but as an adolescent he went through rebellious phases like any other – styling himself on English youths, smoking in secret with a Muslim friend, seeing girls other than his wife and eating meat (forbidden to strict Hindus).

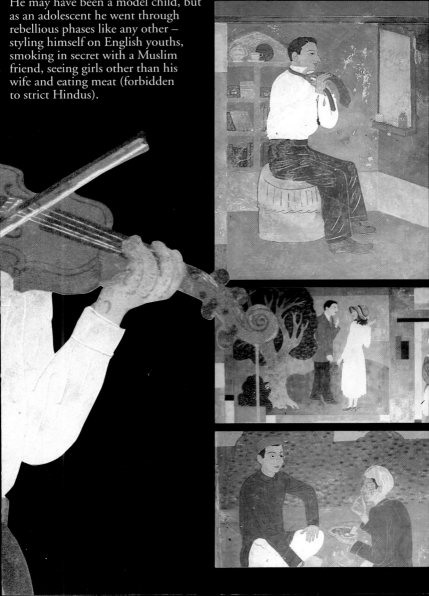

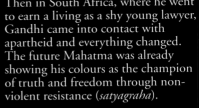

Then in South Africa, where he went to earn a living as a shy young lawyer, Gandhi came into contact with apartheid and everything changed. The future Mahatma was already showing his colours as the champion of truth and freedom through non-violent resistance (*satyagraha*).

Between 1915, when he returned to India after more than twenty years in exile fighting for the cause of freedom, and 1948, the year of his assassination, he was the driving force behind India's long struggle for independence. A small-voiced man with a loincloth and a sweet smile, who used unprecedented political methods to gain what he wanted, Mahatma Gandhi created a new India – a liberated India.

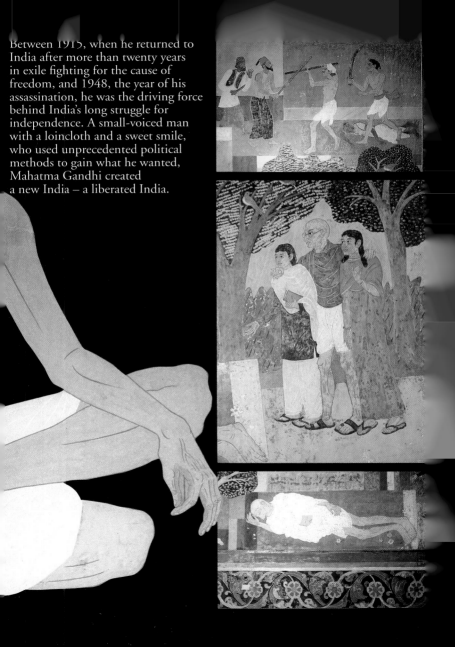

CONTENTS

GANDHI
THE POWER OF PACIFISM

Catherine Clément

DISCOVERIES
HARRY N. ABRAMS, INC., PUBLISHERS

For three centuries India had been the British Empire's most glorious economic asset. This vast territory with its three hundred million inhabitants was guarded by two hundred thousand 'native' and sixty thousand British soldiers. A mere ten thousand officers were in charge of the troops and two thousand rigorously trained Indian civil servants were responsible for overall administration.

CHAPTER 1
EARLY LIFE

Left: Queen Victoria in front of St Paul's Cathedral on the occasion of her Jubilee in 1897. Right: elephant, symbol of the power of the maharajahs.

It was in 1600 that William Hawkins, captain of the
East India Company vessel the *Hector*, landed at Surat,
near Bombay, and started trading. 'Commerce, not
colonization' was the newcomers' motto, but the passion
for conquest proved stronger and the governor generals
representing the East India Company gradually pushed
further into each of India's princely states in turn.
By the early 19th century the company was no longer
just concerned with trade; in effect it ruled over large
areas of India. In 1858 it ceased to exist; the Empire
had come into being and Queen Victoria, soon to
receive the title Empress of India, assumed sovereignty
over India.

No one has given us a better description of India
at that time than Rudyard Kipling (1865–1936) in
his famous *Jungle Book* (1894) and *Second Jungle Book*
(1895). A fact to bear in mind, however, is that the
wild child, Mowgli, ends his days (in 'Mowgli's First
Appearance') as a forest warden on a game reserve,
receiving a pension from Her Majesty. For company
he has his four wolf brothers – the only vestige of
his former life – plus a Muslim wife and children,
and he lives happily enough, still king of the jungle,
but in the service of an even more powerful master.

Queen Victoria, Empress of India (though she never visited the country), photographed (left) in England in 1893 with one of the viceroy's personal staff. His palace in Delhi is now the presidential palace, but staff still wear the same costume.

Opposite: the viceroy's summer residence at Simla in the Himalayan foothills, painted in 1893.

Rudyard Kipling, author of *The Jungle Books*, was born

in India in 1865. He worked there as a journalist from 1882 to 1889. In 1907 he was awarded the Nobel Prize for literature. He died in 1936 and his ashes lie in Westminster Cathedral.

In Kipling's stories Simla, the viceroy's summer residence and a hillside resort for English families retreating from the heat of the plains, is the setting for doomed love affairs between desperate young men and icy, beautiful women who remain out of reach. India casts its spell and the young men pay with their lives, supposedly succumbing to fevers or snake bites, engaging in furious fights or turning into wild animals through some medicine man's magic.

The English seemed to be ensconced in India for good. They had no social contact with local people; Indians were refused admittance to the clubs and did not enter white men's houses, nor were they allowed to appear in national costume in Simla's main thoroughfare. On the one hand there were the sahibs, the master race, drinking their whisky and donning smoking jackets for dinner; on the other the vast masses of the local population, whom the English regarded as passive, illiterate and underdeveloped. The better-off and better-educated Indians had the opportunity to study in Britain and learn the benefits of wing collars and English law. It was a dream of the young to be able to play golf, tennis and cricket in the company of these pink-skinned men who sweated in the heat and were struck down by dysentery and malaria, but whose supremacy in India was never questioned.

India, also known as the 'subcontinent', was governed first and foremost by religious laws – not those of a single religion, but of six major religions and a host of minor sects

The key word of the Hindu religion is destiny. Each of us, it asserts, is born into his rightful place in the world, into a caste from which escape is sacrilege, punishable by excommunication. A person's sole responsibility is to follow his *dharma*, his destiny, and after death (regarded by Hindus as an irrelevance) he may hope to be reborn into a superior caste. The ultimate goal – to which only ascetics can aspire – is not to be born again at all, but to experience the total dissolution of the self.

As well as the territories belonging to British India there were 565 princely states governed by either Hindus (maharajahs) or Muslims (*nawabs* or *nizams*). Not all these feudal lords were despots, but they tended to be immensely rich and to lavish this wealth on various pursuits, such as the search for precious stones, regarded as possessing magical powers. Some commissioned ivory carpets made from pieces of elephant tusk; others, clothes woven with golden thread; some celebrated with great pomp and ceremony the 'wedding' of their pedigree dogs, and all without exception adored luxury motorcars. Tiger hunting (opposite below) was also a popular pastime. Today in India there is a ban on killing all but man-eating tigers, and an animal's danger to man has to be proved before the killing is authorized. The British shared the Indian princes' predilection for hunting (opposite above) – while the Indian princes adopted the British craze for golf, polo and cricket: the cartoon by Spy (this page) shows the maharajah K. S. Ranjitsinhji in full cricket regalia.

The other major Indian religions all display the
influence of Hinduism in both its tolerant and its
fanatical aspects, and its allure derives from the millions
of gods it attaches to every province of life. Buddhism
and Jainism hoped, however, to reform the strict rules
of Hinduism, and central to both these religions
are the concepts of nothingness, impassivity,
non-violence and the obliteration of self.
Sikhism, which followed, sought to
establish the existence of one
god, and, in the face
of persecution by the
Moguls, became
a warrior religion. Since
the dawn of Christianity,
moreover, India has
also been the home of
small communities of
Christians, converted by St
Thomas, who is said to have
disembarked on India's western shores among the

lagoons and giant coconut palms of Kerala. Earlier arrivals still were the sun-worshipping Parsees from Persia and those Jews who left Palestine for India prior to the destruction of the temple at Jerusalem. While Hindus, Sikhs, Christians, Parsees and Jews, along with several million aboriginal adherents of an animistic religion, all coexisted in relative harmony, one religion that would not accept compromise stood out from all the rest: Islam. It spread across India in successive, rival waves from the 8th century and the Mogul

Empire was to dominate India until its power finally declined in the face of British supremacy. The Moguls left behind a rich legacy, including a rigorous architectural style, vast and ornate mausoleums, lively, loud Sufi music, court dances and the Muslim religion itself, which has been locked in permanent conflict with Hinduism ever since.

Hindus worship many gods; they eat no meat or fish, and Hindu women are not obliged to cover their faces. Muslims, on the other hand, avoid wine and pork and their womenfolk wear veils.

One of Delhi's several hundred mosques (above). Many of India's architectural masterpieces, its mosaics of pink sandstone and white marble and its domed palaces (of which the Taj Mahal is the most famous), are located in the north, the stronghold of the Mogul Empire.

Opposite: Bhils, aborigines from central India, one of the many diverse groups of people in the country.

Vishnu, Shiva, Krishna and the rest

The Hindu pantheon is crammed with innumerable gods. Presiding over them is Vishnu (seen here, left, with his companion Lakshmi, goddess of fortune), the creator, who can appear in various incarnations (avatars), divine or heroic. One such avatar is the delightful and immensely popular Krishna, divine hero and god of love, seducer of shepherdesses, seen here (opposite top left) with his favourite paramour, Radha. Quite different from Vishnu is the great and terrible Shiva, god of life and death, whose worship is characterized by asceticism and whose dance (opposite, top right) symbolizes the cycle of reincarnation. His wife Parvati is said to have had a child without his help; Shiva beheaded this son in a fit of jealous rage and Parvati remade him with an elephant head, so fashioning the god Ganesh (opposite below right). A child was also born to Shiva, from his sperm alone: the eternal youth Skanda, typically depicted holding a two-pronged javelin (opposite below left).

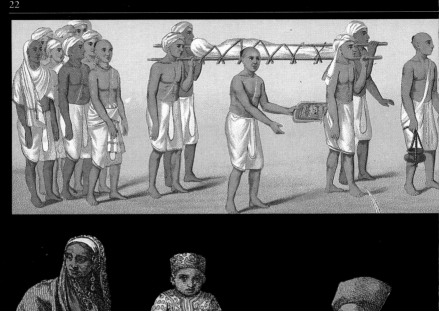

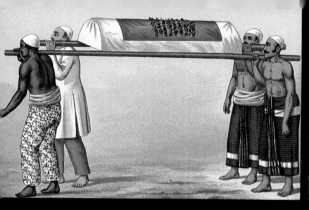

The monotheistic religions: Islam, Judaism, Parseeism and Christianity

Opposite (above) and this page (above left): illustrations depicting, respectively, a Hindu and a Muslim funeral service. The Hindu is being carried on a bier to the river for cremation, while the Muslim is about to be buried. Christians (above right, popular Indian image of St Francis Xavier) settled principally in Kerala and Goa; Jews (left) in Bombay, Calcutta and Cochin (in Kerala), and Parsees (opposite bottom) in Bombay.

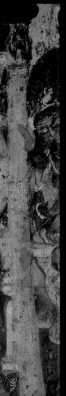

Buddhism, Jainism and Sikhism

These three major religions were derived from the early form of Hinduism known as Brahmanism. Buddhism was based on the teachings of Gautama Siddhartha – seen here (above, centre) painted on a fresco in the Ajanta caves – and was the religion of the Emperor Ashoka, the first ruler to unify India. Both Buddhism and Jainism, which followed it, sought to reform various aspects of Hinduism. Jains emphasize the importance of preserving life in all its forms and a Jain monk will sweep the ground in front of him when he walks in order to avoid crushing a single insect. This page shows (left) a Jain monk meditating and (below left) Jain pilgrims at prayer, with their brushes laid on the ground before them. Like its predecessor, Sikhism sought to reform Hinduism, but also to effect a synthesis with Islam. Nanak, the revered founder of Sikhism, is depicted in a painting (opposite above) and below is a painting of another Sikh guru. To the right of this is a palm leaf drawing depicting the *pari-nirvana* of the Buddha (the total extinction of the Buddha).

Suttee is a voluntary sacrifice (left) made by a Hindu widow who throws herself alive on her dead husband's funeral pyre in order to join him. Although it was officially banned in 1829, it is still occasionally practised today.

In order to incite a riot all a Muslim need do is to hurl some part of a cow into the precincts of a Hindu temple. Conversely, a Hindu throwing pig's trotters over a mosque wall will achieve the same result. Over the centuries, however, the pressures of daily life have led to an uneasy truce between Hindus and Muslims in villages throughout India.

These religious divisions are further complicated by ethnic differences. The northern plains of India are principally inhabited by tall, light-skinned people of Aryan stock, while the Dravidians of the south are a shorter, dark-skinned race that was subjugated by the Aryans in prehistoric times. The east is the home of the Nagas, formerly animists and head-hunters, now converted to Christianity, while in the Himalayas a form of Tibetan Buddhism is practised that incorporates a terrifying array of demons.

Fragmented by the British Raj, India gradually developed a sense of national identity

The majority of British officials had little interest in getting to know the country where they had chosen to serve: their principal concern was to protect themselves and to establish control. Even Indians from the higher castes had little understanding of their own country: to be born an Indian meant being obedient to the British and possibly adapting to their social etiquette and learning to live by colonial laws.

And yet, thanks to the influence of Christian humanist thinking, India was gradually beginning to develop a sense of national consciousness. In the 19th century a number of brilliant intellectuals emerged in Bengal. Among them was Rammohan Ray, founder of a reform movement known as Brahmo Samaj, the 'Society of Believers in Brahma', which sought to persuade the British to ban the Hindu practice of suttee, whereby a wife willingly allowed herself to be burnt alive on her husband's funeral pyre. Mysticism was enjoying a powerful resurgence in Bengal when Gandhi was born in 1869 and the Hindu saint and religious teacher Ramakrishna (1836–86) dedicated his life to the worship of the Mother Goddess of Calcutta, the awesome Black Kali, mistress of both life and death. Ramakrishna's version of the goddess, however, was a smiling synthesis of the demon goddess and the Virgin Mary. His disciple Vivekananda (1863–1902) was the

No Hindu goddess is more terrifying than Black Kali, seen here in a popular 19th-century image. She is the protective deity of Calcutta and her cult is characterized by acts of frenzied ritual; but if Kali is murderous – a goddess created by divine alliance in order to conquer an evil spirit – she also has a kindly aspect as the goddess Durga. Kali-Durga is both life and death, protector and destroyer; she is the joyful, dancing representation of the mother, capable of both nourishing and slaying her offspring. The great 19th-century mystics Ramakrishna and Vivekananda transformed the goddess into a figure with aspects of both Kali and the Virgin Mary, a more modern mother whom Freud himself would have had no difficulty acknowledging.

first to grasp the power of Hinduism as an autonomous religion, but Vivekananda died in a state of mystical fervour at the age of forty, a martyr to his religion.

In 1885, with the blessing of the government in London, the Englishman Allan Octavian Hume founded a party whose purpose was to enable Indians to express their demands in a moderate, democratic fashion. The Indian National Congress, as it was called, conducted its affairs in a polite, gentlemanly manner and its members wore European dress – for how else were they to gain an audience with the sahibs?

The future Mahatma was born into a family which, though well-to-do, belongs to one of the lower castes

Gandhi's home town of Porbandar lies on the Arabian Sea in the northwestern state of Gujarat and most of

Photograph of Gandhi's birthplace (above left) in Porbandar, a small port in the Kathiawar peninsula in northwest India, where a member of the Gandhi family had served as prime minister for six generations. The house was flanked by two temples and lay at the heart of the 'White Town'. In the photograph (above right) Gandhi is seven years of age.

the inhabitants are either fishermen or shipowners. It is a town of white stone houses, temples and alleyways, in a tiny state of the same name where for several generations the Gandhis had exercised the noble office of prime minister. The name Gandhi means 'grocer', however, and the family belonged neither to the highest caste, the literate priestly caste of Brahmans, nor to the military Kshatriyas, but to the third caste, the Vaishyas or merchants. Immediately below them were the Shudras (labourers) and below them the lowest levels of society, the damned souls condemned to live the life of human vultures in the twilight world of the Untouchables.

Mohandas, who was born on 2 October 1869, was the fourth and last son of Karamchand Gandhi's fourth marriage and he grew up in one of those large, many-storeyed Indian houses in which several families coexist, with barely a wall to separate one from another – a situation requiring awareness, respect and a willingness to compromise, and one which Karamchand Gandhi managed well. He was comfortably off and could afford to wear gold jewelry and buy his beloved youngest son an accordion.

His wife Putlibai was a serious, pious woman with high Hindu principles. She belonged to a small sect whose precepts were based on a synthesis of sacred Hindu texts and the Koran, and her daily life was governed by vows and ritual observances, periodic fasting and the practice of tolerance.

The young Mohandas, known as Mohania, was insatiably curious. When he was not slipping, as his sister said, 'like quicksilver' into all the nooks and crannies of his large family home, he would be roaming the streets of the bazaar.

He was fascinated by saintly legends of sacrifice and family devotion, and the picture that emerges is of a happy, kindly, smiling child – one who would climb a mango tree in order, as he himself put it, to bandage the wounded fruit.

The development from child to adult was one he was obliged to make, however, in a single leap.

In orthodox Hinduism only the priestly caste of Brahmans can perform sacrifices, or *pujas*, as the priest is doing in this 18th-century miniature. The Gandhis did not belong to the Brahmans, but to the Vaishyas, the rather lowly merchant caste, and within this to the sub-caste known as the Modhs Banias, the word *bania* signifying throughout India 'a wily merchant'.

As Hindu law dictated, Mohania became a husband, though he had barely reached puberty

At fourteen Mohania was married, as custom dictated, to a young girl whom he had never met. Kasturbai was thirteen and was to prove a wonderful new plaything.

'And oh! that first night,' he exclaimed forty years later. 'Two innocent children all unwittingly hurled themselves into the ocean of life.'

It was with a mixture of delight and despair that Mohania wallowed in those ocean waves. He was passionately in love and gave his young wife no peace, making excessive demands on her in bed and forbidding her to go out, even for walks or to play with her friends. The couple argued and Mohania rarely laughed any more.

He was still growing up and was as curious as ever: he experimented with datura, a plant with narcotic properties, and, as a protest against his lack of independence, decided to commit suicide with a friend. Three Belladonna seeds failed to produce the required effect, but Mohania's rebellious phase was not yet over.

Depicted below three years after her marriage in 1883, Kasturbai was only thirteen years old when she married Mohandas Gandhi in a Hindu wedding ceremony such as the one above.

Mohandas Gandhi, seen here (left) at the age of fourteen with his brother Laxmidas, was the most devoted of Karamchand's sons. As a small child he was fascinated by the story of King Harishcandra, tested by the gods like Job in the Old Testament. The king donates his worldly goods to a Brahman, becomes a slave and gives up his own son, but the gods finally reward his devotion by restoring to him all that he has lost. Another story that moved the young Gandhi was one about a young man called Shravana who carries his two blind parents on his back until he dies of exhaustion. The lament sung by his parents was a piece of music that the future Mahatma frequently played on the accordion given to him by his father.

He became a close friend of a young Muslim boy, Sheikh Mehtab, who persuaded him that if he wanted to grow big and strong like an Englishman he had to eat meat. They used to smoke cigarettes together in secret. Mehtab also tried to lead Mohania astray, without success, by taking him to a brothel once. The young Gandhi was extremely possessive and fiercely jealous where Kasturbai was concerned, without any need to be.

The young husband and model son pursued his secret escapades while promising himself that he would 'reform' his Muslim friend. Mohania's family loathed Sheikh Mehtab. As Sheikh saw it, he was simply trying to make a real man of Mohania.

It was only when his father fell gravely ill in 1885 that Mohania recovered his sense of responsibility, but despite his son's ministrations – the massages and the bandages applied with a mother's loving care – Karamchand Gandhi did not recover. One night Mohania slipped out, overcome with desire for his wife (who was already pregnant). An uncle took his place at the sick man's bedside, but while the young couple were making love a servant came to tell Mohania that his father had died.

When his own child also died, Mohania felt the full weight of adulthood. He was bitterly remorseful, blaming himself for the death of both his father and his baby. He was sixteen years old. Two years later, after finishing his studies, he decided to go to England to study law. His mother resisted the idea, protesting that England would interfere with his Hindu principles and his vegetarianism. A compromise, proposed by a family friend, was finally reached when, in the presence of his mother, Mohandas solemnly vowed not to touch wine, women or meat.

He was on the point of leaving when members of his caste at Porbandar assembled to demand that he cancel his departure, as Hinduism could not be practised in England. He resisted and was excommunicated. 'This boy shall be treated as an outcast from today,' they declared. 'Whoever helps him or goes to see him off at the dock shall be punishable with a fine of one rupee four annas.' Hindu laws are not to be taken lightly.

To all appearances the umbilical cord had been severed, and yet it was in England that Mohania learnt what it was to be Indian

In 1887 he sailed across the 'black water', relieved to have escaped his intense passion for his wife, and in London he found he had everything to learn: not just the law, but also social etiquette – how, for example, to eat with a knife and fork and in particular how to dress. Mohandas took it into his head to become a perfect dandy and when he stepped off the ship he was wearing an immaculate white flannel suit that caused several heads to turn. Once in London he began sporting ties and top hats and neatly dressing his hair.

In his autobiography Gandhi describes his father, seen above, as an irascible man 'given to carnal pleasures'. When he was already nearing fifty Karamchand had married a girl of eighteen, although his third wife was still alive and suffering from an incurable illness. The young Gandhi was passionately attached to his father. At fifteen Gandhi reduced him to tears by confessing some minor theft. As Gandhi wrote: 'Those pearl-drops of love cleansed my heart, and washed my sin away.' And yet the boy was making love to Kasturbai at the moment of his beloved father's death.

His passion for learning was boundless – he danced, learnt French and played the violin, looking set to become the perfect English gentleman.

It was through his observance of his third vow, concerning meat, that Mohandras' conversion to things Indian began. He approached the question of diet with the same enthusiasm that he had put into being a husband and subsequently a dandy. He joined the

Gandhi with other members of the Vegetarian Society in London in 1890.

Vegetarian Society in London and began economizing more and more on his expenses – food, public transport and finally lodgings (though never clothes). He ate very little, walked a great deal and lived in surroundings of calculated poverty.

As for women, he was far too timid even to approach them. He did lie, however, about what he now deemed to be a shamefully early marriage, describing himself as a bachelor – a pretence he was able to keep up until the day an ageing Englishwoman took it into her head to marry him off and he was obliged to confess.

When eventually he felt the first stirrings of desire for another woman he escaped just in time, describing how his heart thudded and his limbs trembled and he felt like an animal that has narrowly escaped the hunter. Sheikh Mehtab had lost: Mohandas was a Hindu.

It was in England that he really first encountered the idea of God. He had not gone to the temple in India but had lived, as he put it, in 'the Sahara of atheism'. Now he was away from home he read a great deal, enthusing about the New Testament and the Sermon on the Mount and Edwin Arnold's *Light of Asia, or the Great Renunciation* (1879) on the life and philosophy of the Buddha, but also devoting himself to the Bhagavadgita, a key Hindu text teaching renunciation of the material world. Mohandas was overwhelmed. His fascination for England had led him back to origins whose importance he had never suspected, and it was in London that he

By the time he left London (above, in the 1880s) Gandhi had discovered his Indian roots; but he had also learnt how to negotiate the law, and throughout his life his legal skills never deserted him.

This 18th-century miniature from south India shows a scene from the Bhagavadgita, a Hindu poem composed about 300 BC and forming part of the epic Mahabharata. This scene, the most famous of all, takes place on the eve of a legendary battle, which is being waged on behalf of Earth, who has complained to the gods that she is overburdened. Krishna, the divine charioteer, is explaining the truths about the cosmos and reincarnation to the hero Arjuna, who is due to lead one of the armies next day but is reluctant to fight against his kinsmen and relations. The purpose of Krishna's 'divine' lesson is to convince Arjuna of the futility of life and the vanity of the physical body, and the pointlessness therefore of human feelings. Arjuna is amazed by the visionary appearance of the god in the guise of his charioteer; he consents to go to war, and Earth is relieved of her burden.

experimented with the idea of being a Hindu, and in particular an Indian.

In 1891 Mohandas was called to the Bar and now returned to Bombay not just a fully qualified lawyer, but transformed in other respects too. He had not lost his natural shyness, however, as was demonstrated when his brother Laxmidas asked him to plead his case with a British official who had dismissed him. The young lawyer hesitated, finally plucked up his courage and then went about things so badly he got himself thrown out of the building. One thing he had not yet learnt was the art of persuasion.

There was a risk that the official in question might ruin his career and Gandhi decided to take his chances and accept the offer of work with an Indian law firm in South Africa. The contract was for a year; the pay was good, and they were offering him first-class travel. So, once again, he left India. His mother had died while he was in London. He now had two sons; his wife was a fully grown woman, and this second parting was a painful one. Gandhi was going out into the world and out – though he did not yet know it – into battle.

South Africa was also part of the British Empire and thousands of Indian contract workers went out to work there for British and Boer employers. Indian slave labour was more profitable than black slave labour, providing better 'returns': Indians were economical and hard-working and hired themselves out for five-year periods on the farms.

CHAPTER 2

PRACTICAL TASKS: THE MAKING OF GANDHI

Although they had to compete with the wealthier and better-educated Indians for jobs in business and in the professions, the whites tended to regard all Indians, regardless of caste, as coolies (right) who did not have the right to live a dignified life. Opposite: famine victims in India.

It was while he was on his way to Pretoria to conduct his legal business that Gandhi was first made to feel like a 'dirty coolie'. A white man objected to the fact that he was travelling first class and had him thrown off the train with his luggage, so that Gandhi was obliged to spend the night on the station platform at Maritzburg, rigid with cold and indignation. It was at this stage that his political ideas first began to take shape. Indeed, Gandhi later regarded the incident as a formative experience in his career.

The shy young lawyer was able to negotiate a compromise that satisfied both parties in the case, and, with his business in Pretoria concluded, he assembled the local Indian population and encouraged the people to take a close look at the conditions under which they were living. He organized one protest meeting after

another and it was through his efforts that Indians finally obtained what had at first seemed impossible – the right to travel first class, provided they were 'properly' dressed.

Now that his initial shyness had been overcome Gandhi was a successful lawyer, effectively arguing in defence of civil liberties, and when his contract came to an end a year later his colleagues gave a party in his honour. It was during this party that Gandhi's eye fell on a newspaper column revealing that the government in Natal was preparing to deprive Indians of the right to elect members to the legislative body. Gandhi had been on the point of returning to India, but he was asked to stay on another month and he accepted.

From the start Gandhi attracted a following of sincere people who shared his ideals and his simple lifestyle. This photograph shows him in South Africa in 1905 with the first of a long line of white supporters: Henry Polak (left), a former journalist, and (right) Gandhi's secretary Sonya Schlesin (of Russian origin), who always staunchly refused a pay rise.

'Thus God laid the foundations of my life in South Africa and sowed the seed of the fight for national self-respect'

Within a fortnight he had gathered ten thousand signatures to his first petition and had founded the Indian Congress of Natal. Relying on the force of the written word, he published two pamphlets appealing to the humanitarian feelings of the white population. The white government had just decided that contract workers who wished to work in a free capacity could do so if they first paid a levy of three pounds – the equivalent of six months' pay. Sensing that his stay in South Africa was going to be a protracted one, Gandhi returned home to fetch his family.

Gandhi's image gradually changed over the years – the Anglicized Indian (left) gave way to the 'native' Indian (*swadeshi*) dressed in his white cotton tunic. The Congress cap (right) – still worn by the party today – was identical to the one worn by South African prisoners.

Bombay was suffering from an epidemic of the plague when he disembarked. In the town of Rajkot, where he offered his services, Gandhi inspected the toilets and discovered that the wealthy were more lax in matters of cleanliness than the poor. Hygiene was one of Gandhi's overriding passions and thanks to this new opportunity he could now extend his private obsession to the whole of India. He took advantage of his return home to describe to his countrymen the fate of their fellow Indians in South Africa. He appealed to the press, aware of its influential role, published his 'green pamphlet', met leaders of Congress and won sympathy for his cause – but no more. Responding to an urgent request for his return, he embarked for South Africa in the company of a boat full of Indian emigrants.

Arriving in Durban, the ship was put into quarantine because of the plague risk, but also to prevent the immigrants from disembarking. Gandhi, as their defendant, was held responsible for their arrival and when he stepped on to the quay he was met with a storm of abuse, surrounded, pinned against a railing and bombarded with bricks, stones and rotten eggs. He fell to the ground and would have been lynched if the wife of the police superintendent had not used her open parasol to shield him.

Perturbed by news of these events, Joseph Chamberlain, the colonial secretary in the Conservative cabinet in Britain, demanded that the aggressors be hunted down, but Gandhi made a public statement vetoing such action.

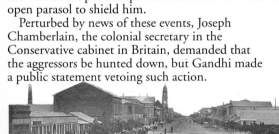

Disarming the enemy meant working on his feelings, not responding to one wrong with another. The Natal government resigned itself to removing from its laws any such discriminatory terms as 'race' or 'colour'. The white population, however, saw things differently and new bills were drafted in which the discrimination was simply veiled. Gandhi knew that the fight was not over; but his generosity had made him famous: 'The Press declared me to be innocent and condemned the mob,' he writes. 'Thus the lynching ultimately proved to be a blessing for me, that is, for the cause.'

With the outbreak of the second Boer War in 1899 Gandhi volunteered to serve as a stretcher-bearer, and so demonstrated his loyalty to England and, as he hoped, the sincerity of his cause

Gandhi founded the greatly admired Indian Ambulance Corps and was awarded a medal; then in 1901 he decided to return to Bombay.

Above: Indians arrive in Durban at the end of the 19th century. They were recruited for (renewable) five-year periods to cultivate sugar cane, a job previously done by the Zulus.

It was in Durban (opposite, c. 1890) that Gandhi was almost lynched by a crowd. To distract the troublemakers the superintendent of police began singing the words of a popular song: 'Hang old Gandhi on the sour apple tree...'

Gandhi called his second ashram (left) Tolstoy Farm in honour of the great Russian writer, whose simple lifestyle on his country estate of Yasnaya Polyana was inspired by ideals similar to Gandhi's own. Gandhi admired Leo Tolstoy's philosophy, wrote to him and received a reply from the elderly writer shortly before the latter's death in 1910.

Just as he seemed set to lead a quieter life, he was recalled to Durban for what he assumed would be another year in South Africa. Chamberlain was due to visit and Gandhi was required to present the Indian community's demands to him. However, Gandhi's glorious war service did nothing to further his case with Chamberlain, and the interview was to prove fruitless.

This time Gandhi set up home in Johannesburg, in the Transvaal, where his life began to change in subtle ways. While he continued to fight his legal battles and advocate a policy of non-violence, he began to perform certain daily tasks that were the logical consequence of his experiments as a child and as a young man in London. Almost as if he were just playing, he began cutting his own hair, washing his clothes himself, cleaning up after he had gone to the toilet – an absolute scandal in Kasturbai's eyes, though he obliged her to do the same, despite her protests that she was a Vaishya, not an Untouchable. Gandhi refused to give way on anything. He reduced their expenses: for one meal a day they simply ate a few dried fruits, dates and nuts, and a mud poultice applied to the belly served in lieu of medications. Gandhi began to fast for his own private benefit, as he would later fast publicly and for the benefit of others.

Working to improve himself was all very well; however, it was now time, he felt, to try and reform others. In Bombay in 1901 his son Manilal had contracted typhoid. A Parsee doctor prescribed

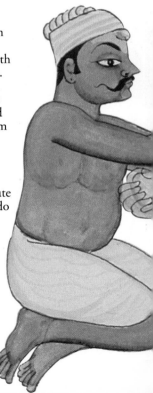

chicken soup and eggs, but Gandhi refused the remedy on the grounds of his vegetarian doctrine. Instead, in anguish, he gave his son boiling-hot hip baths – administering them himself as carefully as a mother – and orange juice diluted with water. The child recovered and Gandhi, now completely convinced of the benefits of natural medicine, gave thanks to God for saving his 'honour'. Still he felt he had not gone far enough. He had just read John Ruskin's volume of social criticism *Unto This Last* (1860), which preaches a return to the simple life. In Ruskin's work Gandhi rediscovered the teachings of the Bhagavadgita. In order to pass beyond a life based on possessions, he resolved to set up a collective farm and 'house of prayer' – the first ashram – in Phoenix, twenty-odd miles from Durban. Its inhabitants kneaded their own flour to make unleavened bread and life in the ashram was governed by rules of monastic austerity. Yet still its formidable director was not satisfied.

The time had come for Gandhi to make his great gesture of renunciation. In renouncing sexual relations, as Hindu custom dictated, he was arming himself for a new kind of combat: civil disobedience or *satyagraha*

In 1906 there was a Zulu uprising in the Transvaal. Gandhi again volunteered to serve as a stretcher-bearer and when the white doctors abandoned the dying Zulus to their fate he did what he could to help them. At the end of the war he was a sergeant-major and had

Gandhi with the Indian Ambulance Corps in 1899, during the Boer War.

Hindu barber shaving a client's head (left). Cutting hair was a job for Untouchables, so that Gandhi's decision to cut his own had greater implications than might at first appear.

Members of the Indian Ambulance Corps at work during the Boer War (detail). Gandhi's support for the British Empire was from the outset a paradox – and one that persisted until 1942. Justifying this aspect of his political philosophy, Gandhi remarked: 'Every single subject of a state must not hope to enforce his opinion in all cases. The authorities may not always be right, but as long as the subjects give allegiance to a state, it is their clear duty generally to accommodate themselves, and to accord their support, to the acts of the state.'

received another medal, and he was now resolved to make a still bigger sacrifice in his life. According to Indian religious custom, a man who has reached maturity, and who has fathered a son to carry on the family name, can take a vow of chastity, *brahmacharya* – a serious, lifelong commitment. On his return from the war Gandhi announced to Kasturbai that he no longer intended to have sexual relations with her. She was quite happy to consent. The purpose of conserving his creative energy would be to channel it henceforth into his spiritual conflicts. Our modern knight was now fully equipped and ready to embark on his own private war.

Shortly afterwards the Transvaal government published an ordinance obliging all Indians to register with the authorities and have their fingerprints taken. If they defied the 'Black Law', as it was known, they could be liable to fines, deportation or imprisonment.

At a rally organized by Gandhi at the Imperial Theatre in Johannesburg on 11 September the three-thousand-strong crowd, at a fever pitch of emotion, vowed to defy

the edict if it became law.

A new type of action was in the making and it needed a new name. One of Gandhi's cousins proposed *sadagraha*, meaning 'steadfastness in a good cause', and from it Gandhi coined the term *satyagraha*, 'firmness in truth'. The exponent of *satyagraha* persisted in

Gandhi in South Africa: (left) dressed as a *satyagrahi* in 1914 and (above) in the same outfit, with Kasturbai. This outfit, invented by Gandhi, was a cross between south Indian dress, a monastic habit and military uniform; the stick, a symbol of militant marches, remained an abiding accessory. By the time these photographs were taken Gandhi had made his vow of chastity and embarked on his path of total asceticism.

saying no, publicly, but without resorting to violence. Gandhi had borrowed this notion of non-violence, *ahimsa*, from the Jain religion, which had a strong following in Porbandar. In terms of human action *ahimsa* was the ultimate metaphysical discipline that encouraged the practitioner to engage in fewer and fewer actions in order to minimize the risk of violence: an approach at which Gandhi was already adept.

Gandhi went to see the new colonial secretary, Victor Alexander Bruce, the ninth earl of Elgin, on behalf of his fellow Indians in South Africa. Elgin promised that the new edict would never become law, but he was being disingenuous: the Transvaal was granted independence on 1 January 1907 and was henceforth free to pass its own laws – which it did. Gandhi's only option was to refuse to register, and he was promptly arrested. He 'respectfully' requested the most stringent penalty, defended his cause by pleading guilty and was put into his first prison – where he felt liberated and happy.

General Jan Smuts (c. 1898), state attorney, minister of finance and defence in the Union of South Africa, and later prime minister of South Africa.

The South African statesman General Jan Smuts (1870–1950) promised that if the Indians would register of their own free will the law would subsequently be repealed. Gandhi duly registered and encouraged his fellow Indians to do the same, but Smuts reneged on his promise and Gandhi was beaten up by two Indians, outraged at what they regarded as his 'treachery'. At Gandhi's behest the registration certificates he had encouraged others to sign were solemnly burned, and once again he found himself in prison.

While in prison Gandhi read the essay entitled 'Civil Disobedience' (1849), written in opposition to the Mexican War by the American writer Henry David Thoreau. Gandhi had also proposed civil disobedience, but so far had achieved nothing.

In 1913 a Supreme Court ruled that only Christian marriages were recognized as legal in South Africa; but this time Smuts had made an error of judgment

As a result of this ruling Hindu, Muslim and Parsee wives were all reduced to the status of concubines and they now joined in the civil disobedience movement. Crossing the border between two provinces without a certificate was a punishable offence and several groups

of 'sisters' deliberately crossed over from the Transvaal into Natal. Those who escaped imprisonment incited the Indian miners in Newcastle to go on strike, and a few months later Gandhi found himself leading an army of five thousand striking miners. The miners stood firm, despite Gandhi's attempts to persuade them to return to work and his description of the harsh conditions of prison life; so a day was fixed when he and his army of *satyagrahis* would cross the borders of the Transvaal minus certificates and get themselves arrested.

Leaving Newcastle, the miners began their solemn march on 13 October 1913. Gandhi supervised the march and, as head cook, distributed the miners' meagre rations. He had already politely informed the government of the strikers' decision and set out his demands – the repeal of the famous three-pound tax that had been his reason for first

General Smuts played an important part in the achievement of responsible government for the Transvaal: the photograph below shows the official announcement in Pretoria (1907). Smuts and Gandhi later paid tribute to one another. In memory of their lengthy confrontation and its happy outcome Gandhi made Smuts some wooden sandals, which Smuts kept in a glass cabinet.

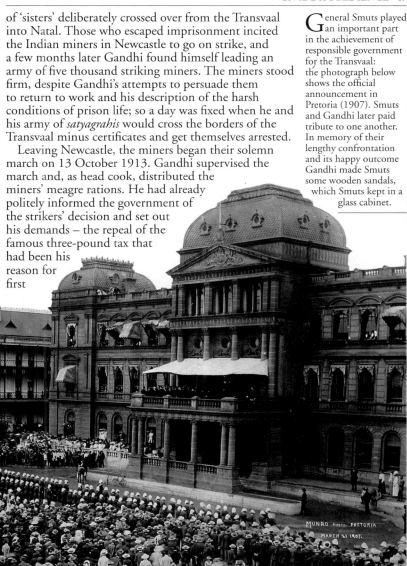

opposing the authorities. On 6 November the marchers crossed the border. On their fourth attempt the police finally succeeded in arresting Gandhi. The movement gathered momentum, with fifty thousand Indians on strike and thousands in prison, and the government in London began to lose patience, horrified by this chaotic turn of events. Gandhi was freed – and was just about to resume his efforts – when he suddenly learnt that the white railway workers had also called a strike.

Gandhi's policy was to avoid humiliating the enemy at all costs and, to general astonishment, he suspended the movement. This piece of 'gallantry' was designed to make Smuts feel moved and he finally began negotiations with Gandhi. New laws were passed by the newly created Union of South Africa to reflect the letters of agreement signed by Gandhi and General Smuts on 30 June 1914. They amounted to a compromise: non-Christian marriages were legalized and the three-pound tax was abolished, but Indian contract workers were not to work in South Africa and controls were imposed on the movement of Indians from one province to another. Gandhi felt he had done what he could to

A total of 2037 men, 127 women and 57 children took part in the Transvaal march – a part of which is seen in the photograph above. They walked barefoot and survived on a little bread – supplied by a European baker – and a little sugar. Once he was arrested, Gandhi pleaded guilty; Herman Kallenbach and Polak testified against him and Gandhi then testified against his friends. According to his code of ethics none of the guilty parties should escape prison – and so avoid setting an example.

Border Volksrust.

defend his fellow Indians in South Africa, and on 18 July 1914 he and Kasturbai set sail for England.

Kasturbai had changed and was heroically following the same difficult and unorthodox path as her husband. She had willingly sacrificed their sexual relationship and submitted to her husband's austere regime, refusing to drink beef stock to treat a serious case of anaemia that had almost killed her; and she had ended up cleaning the toilets like an Untouchable.

Gandhi had been in South Africa for over twenty years and had already made most of the personal sacrifices he was going to in his life. Most recently he had given up milk in order to avoid inflicting further suffering on cows and buffaloes. When two young people from his ashram had committed a sin he decided to fast as a sign of penitence, and as an example to others, thereby setting a precedent for public fasting as a means of social reform. Gandhi was forty-four; over twenty years of painstaking struggles had taught him patience, tactics and eloquence, and familiarized him with prison life; *satyagraha* had been tried and tested. Gandhi was now ready for the real battle.

With regard to the victory in South Africa Gandhi – seen above in 1915 – wrote in *Indian Opinion*: 'It is a force which, if it became universal, would revolutionize social ideals and do away with despotisms and the ever-growing militarism under which the nations of the West are groaning and are being almost crushed to death, and which fairly promises to overwhelm even the nations of the East.'

Gandhi was on home ground now, and his ambition was a straightforward one: to liberate India from imperial rule. And yet he scarcely knew this country where he had spent so little of his life. He had to start afresh – found a new ashram, carve out a political role for himself and discover how best to rouse this sluggish world to action and attack the Empire.

CHAPTER 3

THE ART OF BECOMING A GRANDFATHER

Opposite: Gandhi and Kasturbai in Bombay, 1915.

Right: a crowd in front of third-class railway carriages. In memory of South Africa, Gandhi always travelled third class. Travelling around India by train he was to discover the extent of the hygiene problems from which so many epidemics and endemic diseases stemmed.

Gandhi and Kasturbai were on their way to England when war broke out. Ever faithful to his principles, Gandhi chose to serve as an ambulance driver rather than oppose the Crown in a time of crisis, but a recurrence of pleurisy eventually obliged him to return to India. He was greeted with jubilation and found his country's principal leaders, the Hindu Bal Gangadhar Tilak and the moderate Gopal Krishna Gokhale, readier to listen to him than previously. Gokhale, who was fond of Gandhi and had joined in negotiations with the South African regime, pressed him to observe a year of political silence while he got to know his country again.

Gandhi did as Gokhale suggested, travelling around India in Hindu dress and experiencing the oppressive conditions but also the vitality of Indian village life. On the railways, where he travelled third class, he was exasperated by his fellow passengers – by their rudeness, dirtiness and ignorance. His preoccupation with education led him to visit a new school founded by the Bengali poet Rabindranath Tagore (1861–1941) at Shantiniketan, and run by him – despite Gandhi's attempts to introduce reforms – on indulgent, liberal lines. It was during this visit that Tagore first addressed Gandhi as Mahatma, or 'Great Soul'.

The Mahatma had just written *Hind Swaraj,* his free India manifesto (1908; published in English as *Hind Swaraj or Indian Home Rule* in 1938). While advocating resistance to British rule, Gandhi's programme also stressed the need for self-reform – a reform based on the most enduring of India's traditions, those of its villages.

Between two trips Gandhi founded a new ashram on the River Sabarmati, near the textile centre of Ahmedabad, where he made friends with a wealthy family of industrialists, the Sarahbai. The ashram – a cluster of low white houses and a few mango trees – had a view of the factory chimneys at the nearby prison.

When a family of Untouchables asked to be admitted, Gandhi immediately agreed, despite protests from his followers, and in spite of the risk of losing the charitable grants upon which the ashram depended. The grants were in fact withdrawn, but at the last moment the ashram was saved by a donation from a wealthy visitor: the struggle to liberate India's slave caste had begun.

Rabindranath Tagore (opposite, centre) was from a high-ranking Bengali family, a poet, mystic and altruist who represented one extreme of Calcutta society. The relationship between Gandhi, the man of the West, a member of the merchant rather than the Brahman caste, and Tagore, the man of the East, the Brahman and poet, was a complicated one. While they revered one another – exchanging the names 'Great Soul' and 'Great Sentinel' (Gandhi's name for Tagore) – they were also very different. Tagore was not ill disposed to modern Western civilization; he was a dreamer and a musician, with an indulgent bias, and at his school in Shantiniketan the pupils danced and wove garlands of flowers. Gandhi became obsessed with reorganizing and reforming the school, eager that instead of occupying themselves with flowers the pupils should be taking care of the toilets, the cooking and the housework. Tagore approved of the changes but, as soon as Gandhi left, the school reverted to its gentler lifestyle.

Left: Gandhi in Bombay, 1915.

Above: Bal Gangadhar Tilak, nicknamed Lokamanya, 'he who is respected by the people', Indian nationalist leader and member of Congress. Tilak was as committed to orthodox Hinduism and to the use of violence as Gandhi was to tolerance and non-violence. He claimed autonomy as his 'birthright' – the only slogan for which he is remembered today.

While he was a student in London, Gandhi had discovered the writings of the British theosophist and political campaigner Annie Besant (1847–1933). Gandhi's year of silence was over when Besant, who had just founded a Hindu university at Benares, invited him to speak at the inaugural ceremony on 6 February 1916, in the presence of the viceroy and numerous maharajahs in glittering regalia.

Gandhi spoke, but with such vehemence that his friend Mrs Besant tried to intervene. He attacked the princes for their wealth, the British for their arrogance, the police for their excessive zeal, and went so far as to describe himself as an 'anarchist'. Annie Besant begged him to stop, but he went on, excusing her interruption with a smile – went so far, indeed, that the dignitaries left the platform in disgust and the ceremony had to be suspended. What, one might ask, had happened to that shy student who hardly dared open his mouth in public?

After all the listening and the talking, the time for action had come and Gandhi took up his first cause, championing the rights of the Champaran indigo growers

In the same year, Gandhi took part in the annual session of the Indian National Congress. One day he was approached by a peasant called Raykumar Chukla, who described the exploitation of the Bihar indigo growers by their British landlords and asked him to intercede. Chukla followed Gandhi to his ashram and was so insistent that Gandhi finally agreed to go with him to Champaran.

The system of exploitation was straightforward enough – the farmers were obliged to plant three-twentieths of their land with indigo and give the entire profits to their landlords. Chukla's demands were equally straightforward: he wanted the Mahatma to

Gandhi's Sabarmati ashram, near Ahmedabad.

wipe out 'the stain of indigo'. Gandhi conducted detailed investigations and several days later was taken to court again. He was not alone: thousands of peasants spontaneously gathered outside the court house and so intimidated the magistrate that he failed to press charges – matters in this case moving more swiftly than they ever had in South Africa. Gandhi's fellow lawyers, persuaded of the efficacy of his methods, resolved that they too would face prison in the cause of 'firmness in truth'. A commission was set up by the lieutenant governor, and Gandhi, representing the peasants, demanded that the British planters repay fifty per cent of the sums unjustly extracted from the farmers; the planters proposed twenty-five per cent and Gandhi accepted. The compromise, though not especially favourable financially, represented a crushing moral defeat for the planters – in terms of both their authority and, more importantly, their sense of identity – and they

Annie Besant (above), who founded the All-India Home Rule League in 1916 and devoted her life to the struggle for Indian independence. The school she had opened in Benares (Varanasi) was to form the nucleus of a famous Hindu university. Besant's spiritual quest led her to theosophy, which teaches a blend of Hindu and Neo-platonic doctrines.

Above centre: Gandhi and militants in 1916.

Bihar is a poor rural region in northeast India, at the foot of the Himalayas, just over the border from Nepal. Its people are known for their stubbornness and courage and the region has had its share of social unrest. To reach it from Ahmedabad Gandhi had to cross the entire width of India. His purpose in going there, at the behest of Raykumar Chukla, was to investigate the indigo growers' complaints regarding their British landlords. He was soon to realize, however, that the exploitation of the indigo growers (left) was merely part of an entire system of abuse that gave the colonial powers control all along the line, from the cotton harvest, to the farming of the indigo (for dye), to the manufacture of clothes in British factories using Indian materials and the subsequent sale of the goods in India at prohibitive prices. The situation demonstrated to Gandhi just how thoroughly in his own day and age one country could still exploit another.

would later renounce all rights to the land, which reverted to the peasants. The 'stain of indigo' had been wiped out. The oppressed now had a 'Great Soul' to defend their cause and the whole of India echoed to the name Tagore had given Gandhi.

The way ahead was now clear. Gandhi championed another cause relating to the question of wages and turned fasting into a new political weapon

The new protests – loud and clear this time – were coming from Ahmedabad, where the textile workers were demanding a wage increase. Gandhi agreed to defend their cause, encouraging them to take strike action and extracting a promise from them that they would not return to work until they had achieved their objective. Day after day the strikers assembled under the trailing boughs of the sacred banyan tree, but day after day the position remained unchanged: Gandhi, who had to think of a way to harden their resolve, suddenly announced that he would fast until the workers' demands had been met.

It was a difficult and unprecedented decision, dictated by an 'inner voice' – the irresistible force that was to lead Gandhi to take sudden decisions that were often misunderstood at first. In undertaking to fast for an unspecified period, he was risking his life; but he may have been counting on the friendship of those powerful

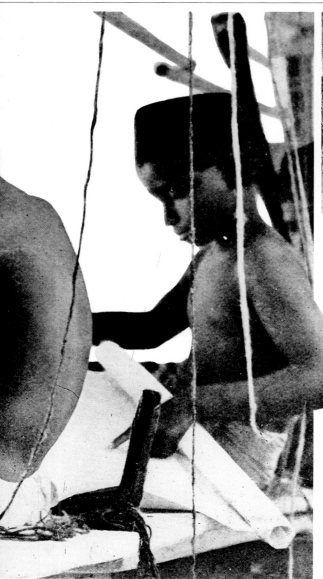

The Ahmedabad weavers (left, in southern India) worked for Ambalal Sarabhai, owner of the largest textile firm in Ahmedabad and the head of one of India's most famous families. Gandhi was a close friend of Ambalal's and his intimacy with the family was such that Ambalal's sister Anasuya actually helped him to organize the strike. Gandhi acted as intermediary throughout, addressing the workers under a large banyan tree (above), while also negotiating with his friends – a conflict of interests that must have put him under an intolerable strain.

textile barons, the Sarahbai. After three days they did indeed give way and a wage increase was agreed.

As with the Champaran compromise, the demands were not met in full. Gandhi was inflexible in his readiness to die for a just cause, but when it came to negotiating conditions his realism matched his swiftness to offer resistance. He agreed to the terms offered as spontaneously as he had decided to fast; and under the sacred tree, christened *Ek Tek* ('keep your promise'), the textile bosses laid on a feast of sweetmeats to celebrate the end of the conflict.

One may wonder what drove Gandhi in a strange and sudden fit to start recruiting for the war effort in 1918 – an activity he undertook with utter commitment, thinking and speaking, as he himself says, of nothing else. It was a 'recruiting madness' and while his mind was in a state of delirium, his body also went into a sudden decline and he became dangerously ill with dysentery, the illness itself barely masking a depression of life-threatening proportions. When the end of the war rendered his efforts redundant and deprived him of his immediate objective, Gandhi turned his thoughts to his physical recovery. What he needed was milk, which he had sworn never to drink, but – at Kasturbai's suggestion – Gandhi decided that the oath did not extend to goat's milk, and he drank this instead. Thanks to the advent of peace, Kasturbai's help and the goat's milk, Gandhi survived his spiritual crisis – and from now on he always kept a goat.

The war was over, but the Rowlatt Acts of 1919 prolonging the restrictions imposed during hostilities had come into force, providing Gandhi with a new spur to action. What Gandhi now proposed was a total suspension of activities throughout India. He politely informed the viceroy of the forthcoming *hartal*, as it was known, and on the prescribed day, 30 March, beginning in Delhi, all the shops and factories closed, children stayed away from school, and life came to a grinding halt.

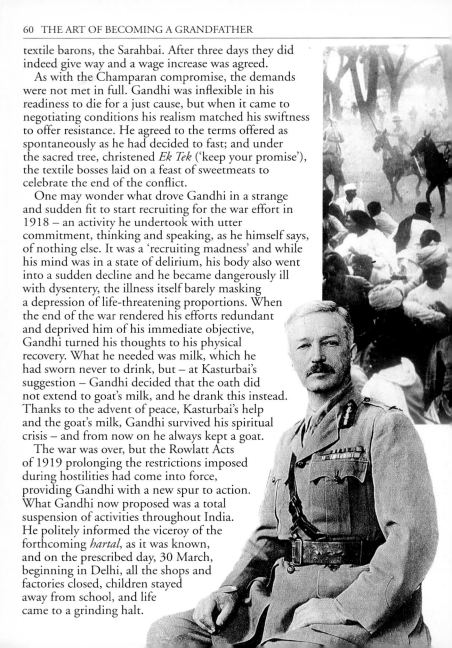

On 13 April 1919 the British army fired without warning on a peaceful gathering of twenty thousand *satyagrahis* in a walled garden at Amritsar, and they continued firing until they ran out of ammunition

General Reginald Dyer (1864–1927) was in charge of the operation, which killed more than three hundred people and wounded almost a thousand others. He had ordered his men to fire into the thickest part of the crowd and calmly informed the horrified commission of inquiry headed by Lord Hunter, senator of the College of Justice of Scotland: 'Yes, I think it quite possible that I could have dispersed them perhaps without firing' but 'I was going to punish them. My

After being relieved of his command General Dyer (opposite) retired to Bristol. Donations from well-wishers living in India and elsewhere provided for a lifestyle that was as comfortable as his actions at Amritsar had been ferocious.

Above: British police break up a demonstration in India, c. 1920.

idea from the military point of view was to make a wide impression.' He was forced to take early retirement.

Devastated by this turn of events, Gandhi accused himself of having made a mistake 'of Himalayan magnitude' and suspended the movement.

On 24 November 1919 he attended a Muslim conference in support of the Khilafat movement, whose existence was threatened by the imminent deposition of the sultan. It was a moving encounter between Hindus and Muslims, united against a common oppressor, and Gandhi took advantage of the occasion to use a new expression: non-cooperation. As Gandhi put it at the time: 'I know that withdrawal of cooperation is a grave thing. It requires ability to suffer. I know that it is the right of the citizen to withdraw his cooperation from the state when that cooperation means his degradation. It is a tangible form of showing one's displeasure at the acts of one's government.'

In 1920 Congress adopted the new slogan. Gandhi returned his medals. Motilal Nehru (1861–1931), father of the future prime minister, gave up his profession as a barrister and hundreds of his colleagues followed his example. Indian institutions took over the function of the universities, now deserted by their students, and villagers, tirelessly harangued by Gandhi, stopped paying taxes and drinking alcohol. Gandhi rallied gathering after gathering – impassioned crowds hundreds of thousands strong – and at the end of each meeting people would strip off their British-made clothes, their trousers and their shirts, and throw them on to a great pile, which Gandhi would light with a smile: once he had burned passbooks, now he was burning clothes.

While the jackets and hats burned to ash, the Mahatma solemnly explained that Indians must now spin their cotton themselves, using the good old traditional spinning wheel, the *charkha*. The Congress flag bore this new symbol and throughout India the *charkhas* began turning.

The spinning and the prayers combined to produce an atmosphere of restless excitement. In an attempt to restore some sense of order, Britain sent its most potent symbol of Empire, Edward, then Prince of Wales and later Edward VIII (1894–1972), to India in November 1921, but Congress boycotted the Prince of Wales in the

The most famous image of Gandhi shows him at his spinning wheel, as he is here (April 1930). During official ceremonies there will always be a group of women spinning in honour of his memory.

same manner that it had boycotted British schools and clothes, and the visit merely provoked a series of riots, followed by arrests. In December twenty thousand Indians, including many prominent politicians, were in prison. It was at this point that a new viceroy arrived in India: Rufus Daniel Isaacs, first Marquess of Reading (1860–1935), a lawyer and son of a Jewish broker. Despite lengthy discussions Gandhi and Reading were unable to reach an agreement and, in response to widespread pressure, Gandhi decided to press ahead and launch a campaign of civil disobedience in Bardoli. The viceroy was informed of the decision, as always, and everything was in readiness when the crowd suddenly lost control and turned on

Opposite: Gandhi in pensive mood.

Edward, Prince of Wales, inspects the regiment of the Seaforth Highlanders (above left) during his visit to India. The regiment was posted to India in 1919 to deal with aborigine poachers. The significance of the Indian boycott of the prince's visit was not lost on the British administration: the protest was a symbolic blow to the very heart of the Empire.

a number of policemen at Chauri Chaura, burning them alive. Horrified by the violence, Gandhi suspended the *satyagraha* movement throughout India, commenting in the 16 February 1922 issue of *Young India*: 'It is indeed million times better to *appear* untrue before the world than to *be* untrue to ourselves.' He was arrested, despite Lord Reading's reluctance, and, demoralized by recent events, demanded that he be awarded the most severe penalty. The judge gave Gandhi a six-year prison sentence, while admitting that his decision cost him dearly in personal terms; but Gandhi was happy: prison was part of his scheme.

His declared profession at the time of his arrest was not 'lawyer', but 'farmer and weaver'.

Gandhi was never happier than when he was in prison gathering his strength and developing his ideas. And he had his own way of firing the enthusiasm of his supporters in his absence: he fasted

Two years later, in prison, Gandhi had an operation for appendicitis and was subsequently released. In his absence the non-cooperation movement had ended. Lawyers had returned to the Bar and students to their

English institutions. More importantly, Kemal Atatürk's secularization programme in Turkey had halted the Khilafat movement and serious hostilities had broken out between Hindus and Muslims. Gandhi looked for a way of stemming the tide of violence threatening to

Sometimes Gandhi was in prison himself; sometimes he visited others in prison, as here (opposite, in Calcutta, 1937?). As he saw it, the prison bars that divided the *satyagrahi* from the outside world were not a barrier, but the symbol of inner freedom and a source of energy.

Gandhi, seen here (below left) in his ashram at Sevagram, regarded prison as both a sanctuary and a place for reflection. It was part of the pact he made with his followers: a *satyagrahi* should not only know, but also love the experience of imprisonment. Today old 'freedom fighters' sometimes express indignation at what they see as the fickleness of modern Indian youth – a youth that avoids prison and is fearful rather than eager at the prospect of imprisonment. Thanks to Gandhi prison became a powerful symbol and there are those who maintain that nothing less than ten years in prison could qualify one as a true *satyagrahi*.

sweep across the country. His answer was to fast for twenty-one days until a reconciliation could be effected between the two communities. While he fasted, two Muslim doctors kept a close eye on him and on the last day of his fast the principal leaders of both Hindu and Muslim communities gathered at his bedside: for the moment Gandhi had won. He now began travelling around India, attracting crowds of adoring supporters wherever he went and never enjoying a moment's peace – a situation he exploited to talk about homespun cotton, *khadi* (his trademark), and collect jewelry from the women and children. It was 1925, the year he was elected president of the Indian National Congress.

The urge to fast a second time – for himself, rather than for a political cause – was prompted by his inner voice. 'This fast has nothing to do with the public,' he wrote in the 3 December 1925 issue of *Young India*: 'I am public property, it is said. So be it. But I must be taken with all my faults. I am a searcher after truth. My experiments I hold to be infinitely more important than the best-equipped Himalayan expeditions.' At the end of his fast he handed over the presidency of Congress to the poetess Sarojini Naidu (1879–1949) and withdrew from national politics for a year.

In 1927 Gandhi ended his year's silence and began organizing rallies again. He had three new themes: opposition to child marriages (of which he had first-hand knowledge), the protection of the cow and the promotion of Hindustani as India's national language in place of English. He held up to seven meetings a day, sometimes in silence, simply standing in front of the crowd with his hands clasped.

The spinning-wheel motif (below) that decorated the Congress flag.

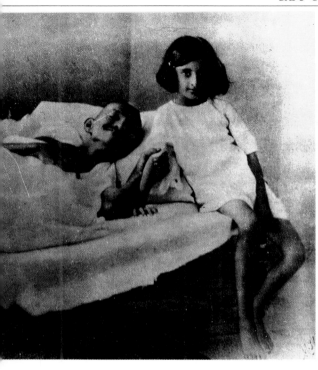

Gandhi with the young Indira Gandhi (1917–84) shortly after breaking the fast that had succeeded in reconciling Hindus and Muslims in 1924. Indu, as she was known, was the daughter of Pandit Nehru, Gandhi's most faithful disciple (and an atheist). She was elected prime minister of India in 1966 and was herself assassinated in 1984.

Most remarkable of all the many women in Gandhi's entourage, the poet Sarojini Naidu (opposite), the 'Nightingale of India', as he called her, was famous for her religious militancy (and also for the beauty of her silk saris, which she even wore in prison). In between spells in prison she had numerous love affairs and was a member of the *satyagraha* movement from its inception, joining in the salt march and taking over, with Gandhi's son, when Gandhi was imprisoned: she led the massive army of *satyagrahis* straight to the police waiting to assault them with batons. Naidu, who christened Gandhi 'Father of the Nation' and 'Mickey Mouse', ended her days as first governor of Lucknow after independence.

However, he was doing too much and had to stop working when he finally collapsed from exhaustion.

In October, after a delay of more than eighteen months, the new viceroy, Edward Frederick Lindley Wood, Baron Irwin (1881–1959), summoned Gandhi to announce the forthcoming arrival of a commission led by Sir John Simon (1873–1954). Not one Indian was included in the commission, whose task was to write a report about India, and it was met in Bombay with black flags and demonstrations. It was high time that Gandhi re-entered the political fray, since the youthful leaders who were preparing to take over from him were 'moderns' who had little belief in his policies of non-violence. Mohandas 'Great Soul' Gandhi was now sixty and throughout India he had recently acquired another name: Bapu, 'Grandfather'.

Gandhi had conquered India in a flash. The smiling old man in his short loincloth and immaculate white shawl of homespun cotton had become a legendary figure in his own lifetime, winning the hearts of millions. He had the mischievousness of a child and the grave authority of a time-honoured Hindu sage. He was not just a Hindu, politician or mystic; not just a merchant, Brahman or warrior: he was all these things at once. Gandhi embodied the very spirit of India.

CHAPTER 4

THE YEARS OF GLORY

Gandhi (opposite, c. 1930) was trailed by photographers eager to take a picture of the future founder of the nation, and his image, reduced to its essentials – bald head, steel-rimmed glasses and moustache – appeared on the 'Boycott British Goods' stamp (right).

It was at Bardoli that the Mahatma had suspended the
satyagraha movement; so it was symbolically fitting that
the movement should be resurrected there. In 1928
87,000 members of the local population rejected a tax
increase of twenty-two per cent and a former lawyer
and mayor of Ahmedabad, Vallabhbhai Patel,
orchestrated the resistance. Despite the seizure of
livestock, land and household goods, Bardoli held firm,
and on 12 June 1928 Gandhi declared a *hartal* in
support of the movement. On 6 August the government
gave way, releasing prisoners and returning the
confiscated lands, livestock, carts and household goods.
The taxes remained at their original level.

There were some, however, among the younger
generation who were impatient with Gandhi's methods.
Outbreaks of violence were met with further violence
and offenders were beaten with the long, heavy batons
known as *lathis*. When Congress reassembled in
December 1929 Subhas Chandra Bose and others
called for 'civil war' and a declaration of independence.
Gandhi finally managed to persuade Congress to grant
the British Raj a period of one year's notice (though
he had originally fought for two): on 31 December
1929, if nothing had changed, Gandhi would
proclaim independence.

In the interim he travelled around the country,
organizing rallies. The violence continued. Bhagat
Singh, a Sikh, already famous for an earlier action, threw
two bombs into the Legislative Assembly hall in Delhi.
The situation was becoming untenable and Irwin cast
around for ways to halt the terrorism. In October 1929,
without consulting the government in London, he
solemnly promised Congress a Round Table Conference
with its first Indian delegates. The answer, as he saw it,
was for India to become a dominion. On 23 December,
a week before the fateful day fixed by Congress, Gandhi
met Irwin. That morning a bomb had exploded under
the train taking the viceroy back to Delhi. In the event
Irwin was unable to promise anything and withdrew
his proposal since both the House of Commons and
the House of Lords had rejected the conference idea
out of hand. At midnight on 31 December, as
promised, Congress proclaimed India's independence.

Police attack demonstrators in Bombay, 1932. 'Civil disobedience' campaigners were met with beatings and arrests, and street scenes like this were not uncommon. Political suspects resolutely pleaded guilty and both men and women eagerly submitted to their prison sentences.

India awaited its instructions from Gandhi: all he had to decide was the place, time and means.

In answer to Tagore's question in January 1930 Gandhi replied that he remained in complete darkness, though he had been desperately applying his mind to the problem day and night

In the midst of all this uncertainty the journal *Young India*, edited by Gandhi around this time, carried an article entitled 'If I am Arrested', devoted to the British salt tax. On 2 March 1930 Gandhi warned the viceroy that a *satyagraha* was scheduled for nine days' time. No one yet knew what he had in mind.

On 12 March Gandhi set off from Sabarmati armed with a pilgrim's stick and accompanied by seventy members of his ashram.

As he walked he preached his usual messages about spinning, about *khadi*, child marriages, alcohol – and, in passing, told people to ignore the salt laws – and for an hour each day he and his companions worked at their

Gandhi (aged sixty) was joined by close friends on the salt march in March 1930. They included Sarladevi Sarabhai, the wife of the owner of the textile firm where Gandhi organized a strike; her son Vikram, who was later responsible for the development of India's nuclear programme; Sarojini Naidu wearing a silk sari and carrying a garland of flowers; and, of course, the Nehrus – old Motilal and his son Jawaharlal. Sardar Patel, who was the co-organizer of the march with Gandhi, was unable to join them because he had been arrested. Jawaharlal Nehru commented, before he was arrested, that their home-distilled salt was fairly disgusting; what mattered to Gandhi, however, was not the taste of the salt, but the taste of freedom.

spinning wheels. Villagers flocked to join them as they passed; three hundred village heads abandoned their duties in the name of non-cooperation, and when they arrived at the coast, at Dandi, the marchers were several thousand strong.

They had been walking for eighty days, but Gandhi had refused to ride the horse brought for his use, or to resort to a cart like some of the others. He was as bright

MAIN PLACES AND EVENTS IN GANDHI'S LIFE

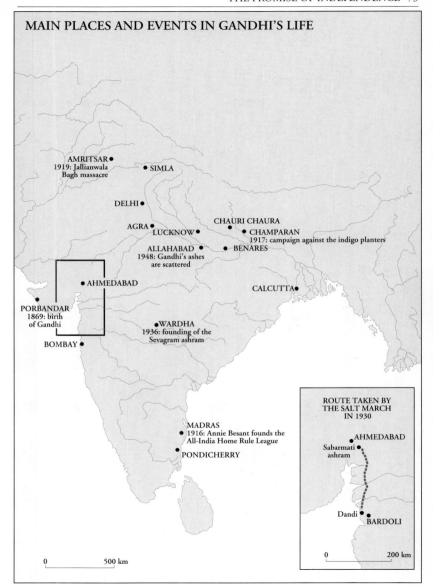

AMRITSAR
1919: Jallianwala
Bagh massacre

SIMLA

DELHI

AGRA

LUCKNOW

CHAURI CHAURA

CHAMPARAN
1917: campaign against the indigo planters

ALLAHABAD
1948: Gandhi's ashes
are scattered

BENARES

AHMEDABAD

CALCUTTA

PORBANDAR
1869: birth
of Gandhi

WARDHA
1936: founding of the
Sevagram ashram

BOMBAY

MADRAS
1916: Annie Besant founds the
All-India Home Rule League

PONDICHERRY

ROUTE TAKEN BY
THE SALT MARCH
IN 1930

AHMEDABAD

Sabarmati
ashram

Dandi

BARDOLI

0   500 km

0   200 km

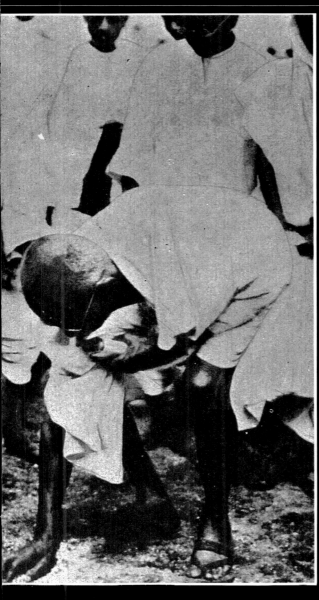

The salt march

Scenes from the salt march – the most significant episode in Gandhi's entire career – including (this page) Gandhi gathering salt on the beach at Dandi, 6 April 1930. It was an event closely followed by both the Indian and the international press and captured in images all the more memorable for their extraordinary simplicity. In 1988 Rajiv Gandhi, the prime minister, retraced Gandhi's steps from the ashram at Sabarmati to the coast. Gandhi maintained that he and his fellow marchers were 'marching in the name of God'. There were seventy of them at the outset, several thousand by the time they reached the sea. They stopped several times a day for meetings and spinning sessions, and along the route villagers, kneeling to pray as Gandhi passed, strewed branches and hung garlands and flags displaying India's future colours. On the edge of the ocean Sarojini Naidu proclaimed 'Long live the liberator!' and Gandhi's first handful of salt was sold to the highest bidder for 1600 rupees.

'Minus fours'

Gandhi responded with good humour to those who welcomed him to London in 1931. He was most amused by some of the responses he received: for example, when a child came and held his hand and called him 'Uncle Gandhi', or when another asked him what he had done with his trousers. To one journalist enquiring about his loincloth – a subject which the British found endlessly fascinating – he replied that Englishmen wore plus fours and he wore 'minus fours'.

as a button and after a night spent in prayer he performed the most famous action of his legendary career: he bent down to the water's edge and picked up a handful of salt.

Thousands of peaceful demonstrators then began gathering handfuls of salt – though to do so was totally illegal – and India was swept by salt madness. Contraband salt was sold in the villages and towns, and the arrests began. There were a whole series of violent incidents, with mounted police in one instance charging a group of demonstrators, who only managed to save themselves from being trampled by lying flat on the ground. Soon there were sixty thousand Indians in prison. On 5 May 1930, a month after his historic gesture, Gandhi was arrested, to his great delight: he could now get some sleep.

There was one thing that remained to be done. Gandhi asked his son Manilal and Sarojini Naidu to launch a peaceful 'attack' against the Dharasana salt works. On the prescribed day, 21 May 1930, two thousand five hundred unarmed volunteers confronted the four hundred policemen guarding the factory. In the bloody scenes that ensued the police killed two demonstrators and wounded hundreds, but as each row fell a new one came up behind to

Gandhi at the second Round Table Conference (left) in London in 1931. He had predicted that victory would be won outside the conference room, by sowing the seeds, as he put it, that would one day sweeten the British attitude, and every detail of his visit was designed to gain the sympathy of the British public – even the goat which came over with him on the boat and provided his daily supply of milk. He stroked children's cheeks; he met factory workers; he talked to the poor; and he even took tea with the king – still dressed in his sandals, his loincloth and his big shawl.

Opposite top: British policemen outside a prison in Bombay around 1930.

Opposite below: an Indian Communist calls for independence for India during May Day celebrations in London in the 1930s.

replace it. Webb Miller, an American correspondent, reported the whole affair for the United Press and testified to the world that India was free at last.

Irwin was in a difficult position. In Britain the Labour Party had been in power since 1928 and the British electorate increasingly favoured independence for India. Meanwhile in India itself the troubles continued. The admirable Khan Abdul Ghaffar Khan, a Pathan who had earned the title the 'Frontier Gandhi' for his non-violent methods, had taken Peshawar without a single shot being fired. The army had responded a few days later with machine guns, but a Hindu platoon had mutinied in preference to shooting Muslims. Irwin clearly had no choice but to negotiate with Gandhi in his prison cell – and swiftly.

The first Round Table Conference took place in London on August 1930. Congress was not represented, although the Muslim Mohammed Ali Jinnah (1876–1948) was present. (He had recently resigned his seat in Congress in opposition to Gandhi's policies.) The Labour Party called for a second conference and expressed the hope that it would be attended by members of Congress. Irwin pounced on this opportunity and released Gandhi in January 1931. It was at this official meeting between Gandhi and Irwin that Winston Churchill raged against 'this one-time

Inner Temple lawyer, now seditious fakir striding half-naked up the steps of the viceroy's palace, there to negotiate and to parley on equal terms with the representative of the king-emperor'. Churchill had understood the stakes. Thanks to the Delhi pact signed by Gandhi and Irwin, all Indian prisoners were freed, the manufacture of salt was made legal and Congress would be represented at the second Round Table Conference.

On 29 August 1931 Gandhi, Sarojini Naidu and a few other members of Gandhi's entourage set sail for London on the *Rajputana*. Gandhi stayed in London from 12 September until 5 December in a poor part of the East End, refusing offers of a hotel and the honours extended to him. The British press adored him and followed him wherever he went. He visited textile workers in Lancashire; he met Charlie Chaplin and went to tea at Buckingham Palace, still dressed in his loincloth and shawl, or 'half naked', as Churchill would have said. He met his former adversary from South Africa, General Smuts, again and apologized for the trouble he had caused him. He dazzled all those who heard him speak in Oxford: he won over everyone he met, in fact. The time for complete independence had come, he insisted, so that India and England could be equal partners at last. He was more interested in winning over public opinion and the support of the British themselves than in speaking at the Round Table Conference, where he was made painfully aware of the gulf that lay between his dream of a free, united India and the reality of the country's religious divisions.

During the last session the president described Gandhi as a Hindu, but Gandhi fiercely resisted the categorization. The outcome of the conference was catastrophic: Muslims, Sikhs, Parsees, Christians, Anglo-Indians and Hindus all demanded their own electorates, and by blandly encouraging their demands the conference made sure independence remained an unattainable goal.

It was time for Gandhi to leave. En route he stopped off in Paris, then at Villeneuve in Switzerland, where he stayed with Romain Rolland

Gandhi's salt march had brought him worldwide publicity. Though he may have irritated Churchill, the people of London loved him and he received a warm reception from the textile workers at Darwen in Lancashire on 26 September 1931 (opposite below). He and Charlie Chaplin (opposite top) may not have had much to say to one another, but their encounter was symbolic. The image of Gandhi spinning, dressed in loincloth and shawl (below), is familiar enough – even if this is London and the winter of 1931. More unusually, we see him planting a tree in the East End, where he lived as a student (opposite centre).

(1866–1944), who had written a book about him in 1924 and regarded him as a hero. In Italy Gandhi refused hospitality from Mussolini (whom he described as having eyes like a cat's) but was unable to avoid spending twenty minutes in his company. The Pope would not receive him, but Queen Elena of Italy gave him a basket of figs that she had prepared herself. He arrived home on 28 December, empty-handed, but with his head held high.

A month after being showered with glory in Europe Gandhi was in prison again

Events had taken a disastrous turn while Gandhi was away. Jawaharlal Nehru (1889–1964), son of Motilal, and the Muslim Tasadduq Cherwani were in prison; new restrictions had been imposed on civil liberties; rallies, boycotts and political associations of any kind were outlawed – a Christmas present, as Gandhi described it, from the new viceroy, Lord Freeman Willingdon, who refused to enter into discussions with him. On 4 January – a month after his London triumph – the Mahatma was in prison, along with almost sixty thousand militant Congress supporters. As usual, Gandhi took advantage of the opportunity to rest and study, and he wrote to members of his ashram, heading his letters 'From the temple of Yeravda' – Yeravda being the name of his prison, and a prison simply a temple where one prayed to God.

In 1932 Gandhi used prison for a different purpose. From the newspapers he learnt that the new constitution, which was in its formative stages, was planning to institute separate elections – not only for India's various religions, but also for the Untouchables

It was time to express his indignation and in a letter of 11 March 1932 addressed to Sir Samuel Hoare, Secretary of State for India, he warned that unless the government changed its stance he would be forced to undertake a 'fast unto death'.

On 17 August Britain decided in favour of separate elections for the Untouchables, and on 20 September, at midday, Gandhi began his fast unto death. Gandhi's fellow prisoner Nehru was exasperated, unable to see the

British soldiers arrest some of Gandhi's supporters. The figures are anonymous, but the illustration has succeeded in displaying India's cultural diversity through the differences in their clothes – the Muslims' turbans, caps and fitted coats; the draped garment and distinctive hairstyle of the Christian (far left) from southern India; the white turban and venerable white beard of the Sikh in the foreground. In the distance a classical Hindu temple can be seen. Irwin prided himself on his ruthless campaign, and, in a matter of months, his repressive policies led to the imprisonment of sixty thousand so-called political criminals (a hundred thousand according to some reports).

Overleaf: Indian resistance against the British occupation (page 84) and Gandhi being arrested in Bombay (page 85) – a scene that is a little reminiscent of Christ's arrest in the Garden of Gethsemane.

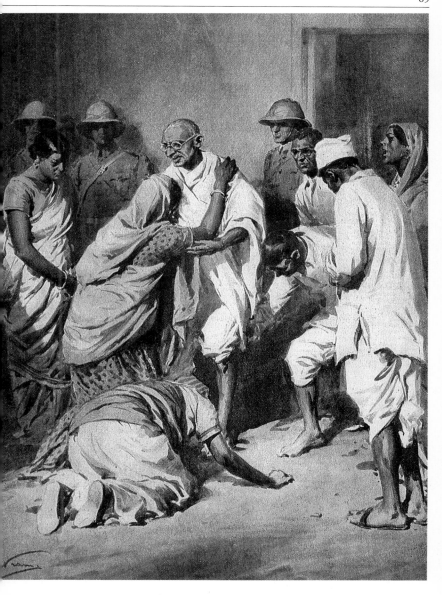

point of this new fast and what the Untouchables had to do with independence.

Nehru soon acknowledged his mistake, and once it became clear that Bapu was risking his life in earnest the whole country was caught up in a state of feverish activity. Prayers were said throughout India, and those Hindu leaders who had escaped imprisonment assembled in Bombay, where they met the leader of the Untouchables, Dr Bhimrao Ramji Ambedkar (1891–1956).

Ambedkar had himself risen from the ranks of the Untouchables to become a lawyer. In his eyes British rule, even Islam – anything – was preferable to the oppressive Hindu caste system, and that an old Hindu – even the Mahatma himself – should be fasting unto death was to him a matter of complete indifference.

Ambedkar was capable, single-handed, of foiling the desperate negotiations to save Gandhi's life. After three days of talks he consented to meet Gandhi, but he demanded 'compensation'. Speaking to him in a whisper, Gandhi, who was already dangerously weak, managed to convince the steely lawyer of his commitment to the cause of the Untouchables, the *harijans* ('children of God'), as he called them. On 23 September Gandhi's blood pressure was rising and he was near to death, but negotiations were still continuing regarding the number of seats to be reserved for the Untouchables. Finally, on 24 September, Hindus and Untouchables signed the Yeravda Pact; but Gandhi refused to break his fast until the text had been formally agreed by the British government. The text was

cabled, arriving in London during the course of the
weekend, and the prime minister, Ramsay MacDonald
(1866–1937), hurried back to 10 Downing Street
to work on it until midnight. In prison Gandhi had
already dictated his last wishes to Kasturbai, who had
been allowed to leave her cell to be with him at the
end. Tagore had arrived from Calcutta. By now Gandhi
could no longer speak.

On the Monday morning of 26 September, a week
after Gandhi had started his fast, London and New
Delhi announced their approval of the pact, and at
5.15 in the afternoon Kasturbai held a glass of orange
juice to her dying husband's lips: the fast was over and
Tagore sang songs of praise in Bengali.

Dr Ambedkar, the
Untouchables'
remarkable leader, a
lawyer with a violent
antipathy to Hinduism.

Untouchables at
prayer (left) in
Bombay during
Gandhi's fast, 1932.

Opposite:
manuscript of
the poem 'Samudra'
('Ocean') from
Rabindranath Tagore's
collection *Puravi*
(*Evening Songs*).
The superimposed
drawing is Tagore's own.

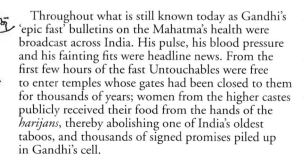

Throughout what is still known today as Gandhi's
'epic fast' bulletins on the Mahatma's health were
broadcast across India. His pulse, his blood pressure
and his fainting fits were headline news. From the
first few hours of the fast Untouchables were free
to enter temples whose gates had been closed to them
for thousands of years; women from the higher castes
publicly received their food from the hands of the
harijans, thereby abolishing one of India's oldest
taboos, and thousands of signed promises piled up
in Gandhi's cell.

The cause of independence may not have been furthered in the short term; but the Mahatma had salvaged the pride of a nation whose oppressor had tightened its grip at the very moment when freedom seemed possible.

Gandhi began to change, almost imperceptibly. Withdrawing from the political arena, he focused on the undramatic day-to-day life of the Indian people and strove to introduce a series of quiet reforms

In 1933 Gandhi was still in prison, having won his most astonishing victory – a victory over his own people, his own community. It was to prove short-lived, since orthodox Hindus are currently seeking to close the temples once more to the *harijans* – and no one is fasting in their defence. While in prison he founded a journal, *Harijan* or *Children of God*, which he edited himself. The first issue appeared on 11 February 1933.

In May of that year Gandhi fasted again for three weeks – for his own benefit this time, to punish himself for thoughts provoked by a young American woman who came to visit him in prison: it was proving a long and difficult struggle to keep his vow of celibacy.

The British authorities released Gandhi on 8 May, on the first day of his new fast, alarmed by its implications, and he continued to fast quietly and without any risk to his life.

In July 1933 he disbanded his Sabarmati ashram and donated it to the *harijans*. He was imprisoned again in August for 'civil disobedience' and fasted again. When he finally retired from public life, having apparently lost interest in politics, it was not entirely clear whether the world

Gandhi in 1938 with Abdul Ghaffar Khan, the 'Frontier Gandhi', so called for his success in persuading the warlike Pathans of India's northwest borders to adopt a policy of non-violent resistance. Ghaffar Khan ended his days in Pakistan, forced to accept the existence of the new frontiers.

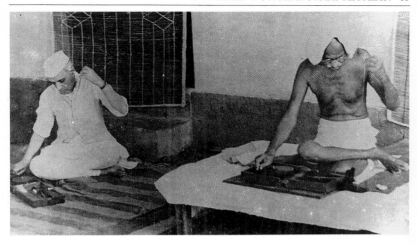

around him was changing or whether Gandhi himself had changed during his epic fast. He concentrated now on reforming India, helping her to discover her eternal roots without worrying about independence. It was as if he regarded independence as inevitable and was anxious to neutralize the dangers that threatened it from within. As far as politics were concerned, Gandhi's spiritual son, Jawaharlal Nehru, could take over where he had left off: Gandhi had set the wheel of destiny in motion; now others could spin it in their turn.

In 1934 he even resigned his seat in Congress. He travelled around India on foot, sleeping under mango trees like a mendicant ascetic or *sadhu* and helping to promote village industries – the manufacture of brooms, matches, toothpaste and toothbrushes – in a move towards self-sufficiency. He was immensely popular and people came from all over the world to see him. He may have retired from the political scene, but he had never been more famous than now.

Whether he had retired for good was another matter. When, in 1938, he accompanied Ghaffar Khan on a journey through the mountain border region where the Pathans live, he told his old friend that he was as powerful as ever and would prove it when the time came.

Jawaharlal Nehru adored Gandhi. Although he may sometimes have sulked over his decisions, he always fell in line in the end, with the devotion of a son. And yet, while Gandhi enjoyed a profound faith that could accommodate doctrinal differences, Nehru was an atheist, who believed above all in progress and science – a fact that did not stop him from quietly getting on with his spinning (above), like his fellow campaigners, in defiance of the British cotton mill monopoly.

By the time the Second World War broke out in 1939 Gandhi had retired from politics. With the years he had become increasingly clear-thinking and radically committed to the cause of pacifism. The Ambulance Corps and recruitment were things of the past. Although horrified by the rise of Fascism, and recognizing in Hitler the very incarnation of violence, his answer to victims of the war – Czechs, Jews, Ethiopians – remained non-cooperation and self-sacrifice.

CHAPTER 5

THE YEARS OF HEARTBREAK

•Refuse to obey Hitler's will and perish unarmed in the attempt. In so doing, though I lose the body, I save my soul, that is, my honour.•

Gandhi, *Harijan*
8 October 1938

EXPLOSION OF U.S.S. SHAW

India's new leaders – Nehru, Maulana Azad, a Muslim member of Congress, and Jinnah, president of the Muslim League – did not share Gandhi's pacifism. Nehru was a materialist, an atheist and an anti-Fascist, and Jinnah was by no means opposed to violence. Only the Pathan Ghaffar Khan, the 'Frontier Gandhi', supported Gandhi's radical stance, and for the first time in his life the Mahatma found that nobody was prepared to listen to him. In the face of Nazi barbarism his methods suddenly seemed disarmingly simplistic and ineffectual. On the question of the Jews in Hitler's Germany, Gandhi wrote in *Harijan* on 11 November 1938: 'I am convinced that if someone with courage and vision can arise among them to lead them in non-violent action, the winter of their despair can in the twinkling of an eye be turned into the summer of hope.'

Gandhi was trapped, torn by an inner conflict that was in the end a 'perpetual quarrel with God that He should allow such things to go on'. As he saw it, it was God who was wrong and he who was right, and Gandhi refused to compromise on the question of pacifism.

On 14 September 1939 Congress (of which Gandhi was no longer a member) condemned the Nazi invasion

From left to right: Gandhi, Nehru, Azad and Jinnah. As India's long struggle for independence was reaching its conclusion three of these men fought desperately to safeguard the unity of their vast country – a goal which they all shared, despite their very different beliefs (Gandhi was a syncretist, Nehru an atheist and Azad a committed Muslim). A Muslim out of patriotism rather than religious conviction, Jinnah alone was committed to carving up the Indian subcontinent to create an autonomous Muslim state – Pakistan.

of Poland and offered Britain military aid in exchange for independence. Gandhi was just about to begin a particularly difficult period of his life. By June 1940 his relations with Congress had become openly hostile. The old campaigner was torn between his horror of war and his horror of Nazism. Reminded of his commitment to the war effort in 1918, he retorted: 'My aim is not to be consistent with my previous statements on a given question, but to be consistent with the truth as it may present itself to me at a given moment. The result is that I have grown from truth to truth.' There was nothing conceited about his answer: he was simply affirming a new perception in his quest for the truth. Yet the truth of 1940 led to a terrible personal defeat for Gandhi.

Congress was waiting for independence. In return it had pledged its immediate support for Britain – the head of an empire that now barely merited the name. In response the viceroy Victor Alexander John Hope, second Marquess of Linlithgow (1887–1952), acting on instructions from Churchill, made it clear that independence was out of the question, but proposed that Congress should be represented on an advisory war committee. In frustration Congress looked again to

The Japanese attack on Pearl Harbor (photograph, above) on 7 December 1941 and America's entry into the war increased the likelihood of India being invaded – and serving as a meeting point between Japanese and German troops. President Roosevelt had clearly understood that India's reluctance to back the Allies was due to Churchill's refusal to compromise over its internal affairs. Roosevelt sent a personal envoy to India and in England meanwhile the Labour Party increased its pressure on the prime minister.

Gandhi as its leader in September 1940, and Gandhi launched a campaign of individual *satyagrahas*, entrusting a number of representatives with the task of travelling around the villages preaching non-cooperation with the war effort. In the spring of 1941 the war threatened to engulf India: Hong Kong had fallen to the Japanese and was followed by Singapore in February 1942, and then by Java and Sumatra. Rangoon, capital of nearby Burma, fell in its turn. General Rommel was advancing on Egypt. A link-up between German and Japanese troops no longer seemed impossible – with the link being forged in India itself. Since Japan had started hostilities, Britain had lost her two principal warships, the *Repulse* and the *Prince of Wales*, and she was powerless to defend her protégé. Linlithgow had all the *satyagrahis* released and approached them with a request for help.

In the United States President Roosevelt was perturbed by news of events in India and demanded a compromise from Churchill. Soon afterwards, on 22 March 1942, Sir Richard Stafford Cripps (1889–1952) arrived in Delhi with a mandate to grant India the status of a dominion with its own constituent assembly – but not until after the war. A third of the assembly's members, moreover, were to be nominated by the maharajahs, who were known to be under British influence. Japan was threatening to invade: the people of India felt both powerless and defenceless – and the British had got the better of them once again.

The extent of the Japanese threat to Asia and the fierce anti–Fascism of India's militant youth frustrated Gandhi's final efforts

For a long time Monday had been a day of silence for Gandhi. On Monday 13 April 1942 – on a day of silence therefore – his inner voice dictated the

Churchill (opposite, in 1939) had served in India as an officer in the fourth battalion of the Queen's Hussars and fifty years later he was still sending two pounds sterling to a former Indian bearer. He loved India and the Empire but growled, 'I have not become the king's first minister in order to preside at the liquidation of the British Empire'. Despite his very real attachment to India he totally despised the leaders of its independence movement – those 'men of straw', as he called them – and Roosevelt's attempts to put pressure on him were met with endless prevarications. To his great chagrin Churchill would eventually be obliged to witness the end of British rule in India.

Above left: riot in India in the 1940s.

Left: Gandhi with Maulana Azad and J. B. Kripalani in August 1942.

watchword: 'Quit India'. In August Gandhi decided to act upon his intuition and launched an appeal for a final act of disobedience, declaring 'Freedom has to come not tomorrow but today.'

Gandhi usually knew how to bide his time and would politely inform his adversary of a forthcoming offensive; but this time he was in a hurry. He appealed for open rebellion, a comprehensive, non-violent revolution, and gave himself three weeks to negotiate with the viceroy and explain his decision. By dawn, instead of the hoped-for freedom, Gandhi found himself – along with all the leaders of Congress – confronting another set of prison walls. Churchill was also in a hurry and since 1935 he had been waiting for the opportunity to undermine the insufferable 'half-naked fakir'.

The old lion growled: 'I have not become the king's first minister in order to preside at the liquidation of the British Empire.' Congress and its supporters became the target for a campaign of brutal repression, and in response the country was swept by a wave of terrorist activities – sabotage, arson, murder – on an unprecedented scale. Gandhi's 'Quit India' had ended in a cruel defeat; but one person who had not been imprisoned was Mohammed Ali Jinnah, president of the Muslim League.

MR. GA

Congre
Rou

**MR. Gandhi, Ma
dent, membe
ral members of
minent local Con;
suburbs early on
cial train.**

NDHI ARRESTED
BOMBAY

Declared Illegal:
-up of Leaders

, Abul Kalam Azad, the Congress Presi-
the Congress Working Committee, seve-
ll-India Congress Committee and pro-
leaders were arrested in Bombay and the
ay morning and taken to Poona by a spe-

There were outbursts of extreme violence when it became common knowledge that the Mahatma was in prison: police stations were set on fire, telegraph lines were destroyed and British officials were attacked. From prison Gandhi corresponded with the viceroy Linlithgow, and each of them blamed the other, in the politest terms, for the wave of criminality sweeping across the country. Gandhi was refusing anything but water and a little fruit juice and Linlithgow could not convince him that this fast was, as he put it on 5 February 1943, an act of 'political blackmail'.

Above left: detail from the front page of the *Times of India*, 10 August 1942.

Below left: an Indian merchant transporting British foodstuffs under police guard.

From August 1942 Gandhi was held at Yeravda in a palace belonging to the Aga Khan, but there was nothing liberating or uplifting about this prison stay, even if the surroundings were more luxurious than previous ones. Kasturbai was arrested as she made her way to a public meeting which she was due to address.

The viceroy, Lord Linlithgow, took it upon himself to demonstrate that Gandhi was responsible for the violence. Gandhi wrote a polite letter denying the accusations, but to no effect. Then he fasted for three weeks. Crowds rallied to his cause once again, and Gandhi nearly died, but the viceroy held firm:

this was outright war, and even fasting, it seemed, was useless now. Gandhi's failures were compounded by personal loss. First his secretary, Mahadev Desai, who was also his adopted son, died; and then, on 22 February 1944, Kasturbai – of acute bronchitis. Right up until the end Gandhi refused to allow the doctors to administer penicillin. After her death he maintained: 'If I had allowed the penicillin it would not have saved her…. And she passed away in my lap. Could it be better? I am happy beyond measure.'

Three months later Gandhi too was desperately ill with malaria and amoebic dysentery. Churchill, for one, would not be sorry to see the old Mahatma die, but realizing that his own reputation might suffer if Gandhi were to die in prison, he released him on 6 May 1944. Churchill was to be disappointed: after a slow recovery Gandhi returned to the fray.

The war was over at last and in 1945 the Labour Party came to power in Britain. One of

Mohammed Ali Jinnah (seen here with Gandhi in 1939) was a wealthy Westernized lawyer who lived in Bombay, in a palace by the ocean. According to the *New York Times* in 1946 he was reputed to be one of the best-dressed men in the British Empire. He was not an orthodox Muslim: he drank alcohol and ate pork, married a Parsee and campaigned in the early days for Hindu-Muslim unity. Then he became obsessed with his 'country of the pure', the world's first Muslim state, and when his daughter married a Parsee he disowned her. In 1944 Gandhi spent eighteen days talking to Jinnah in the hope of changing his mind – but to no avail.

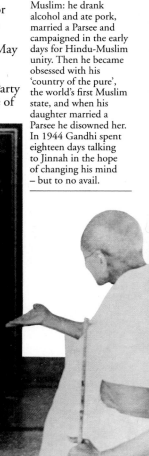

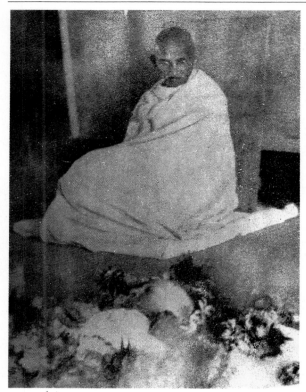

Gandhi at his wife's deathbed in February 1944. Over the years Kasturbai came to be known as Ba, or Mother. She had given up rebelling against her husband's tyrannies and for many years now had shared his vision and worked towards the same goal, speaking at mass meetings and doing her share of time in prison. She was always good at answering him back, however, even if she sometimes failed to grasp the full complexity of his ideas. On his last visit to his dying mother, her eldest son, Harilal, was drunk and reduced her to tears. After her death Gandhi said, 'I cannot imagine life without Ba.... Her passing has left a vaccuum never to be filled.... We lived together for sixty-two years.' However, he declared himself 'happy beyond measure' because he had held her head on his knees as she lay dying. Six weeks later he was seriously ill himself.

the first concerns of the new prime minister Clement Attlee was to grant India independence, a task he entrusted to the viceroy Archibald Percival Wavell, the first Earl Wavell (1883–1950). The goal Gandhi had hoped and struggled for years to achieve was to prove, however, the source of his greatest suffering.

Everything militated against the partition of British India into two independent states, one Muslim, the other non-Muslim

Partition went against geographic, economic and sociological considerations and common sense itself; it was a monstrous vivisection, achieved by the fierce determination of one man, Mohammed Jinnah.

𝕿𝖍𝖊 𝕾𝖚𝖓

𝕬𝖒𝖗𝖎𝖙𝖆 𝕭𝖆𝖟𝖆

RECD. No. L 58.

77TH YEAR OF PUBLICAT

CALCUTTA, SUNDAY, JULY 15, 1945

Editor — TUSHAR KANTI GHOSH

SIMLA CONFER

Before receiving instructions from Attlee, Wavell had released India's main political leaders and opened negotiations with them at Simla in June 1945. Although he was not a delegate, Gandhi went to Simla, where a new enemy was waiting for him – an enemy more severe than Smuts, more tenacious than Churchill and more inflexible than Ambedkar: the Muslim Mohammed Jinnah. Jinnah succeeded in wrecking the conference through his determination to elect all the Muslims of the future provisional government from the Muslim League alone, thereby riding roughshod over the Congress Muslims. His real focus of interest was not the Muslims, or India, but the creation of a new state, his 'country of the pure', Pakistan. No price was too high to achieve his aim. The seeds of division, sown in the 1930s by the Round Table Conference, had begun to sprout.

In March 1946 Sir Stafford Cripps headed another mission to India and the delegates assembled again at Simla, but the discussions were deadlocked because Nehru and Jinnah – not Gandhi and Jinnah – were both quite incapable of agreeing on the smallest concession. The mission examined Jinnah's proposals for partition and demonstrated at length the impossibility of the plan, pointing out that partition would not settle differences between communities; that it would, moreover, completely destroy Bengal and the Punjab and weaken the two countries. Pakistan itself would be divided into two segments separated by more than a thousand kilometres and would be ungovernable as a result. The Cripps mission concluded that a provisional government was needed at the head of a united India.

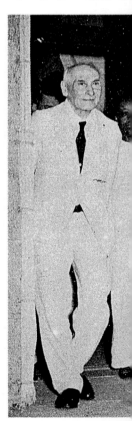

GUINEA GOLD

O N ROY & BROS

Patrika

VOL. Xo. LXXVII. 196.

SHAR 31, 1352, B.S.   3rd DAK EDITION. 2 ANNAS.

ENCE FAILS

Wavell put Nehru in charge of the new government. Jinnah had refused to have any part in it and when Nehru again offered him a ministerial portfolio, Jinnah again refused, announcing that 16 August 1946 would be a day of 'direct action'. Four days later 5000 people were dead in Calcutta and 15,000 wounded. In the Noakhali district of Bengal Muslims were slaughtering Hindus, forcing them to convert to Islam and raping their womenfolk. In Bihar the Hindu majority was massacring Muslims by tens of thousands. India did not yet properly exist, and already it was tearing itself apart. Gandhi no longer had a political role to play and scarcely anyone listened to him any more. Although he was not concerned with affairs of government, he recalled that, by fasting, he had succeeded once before in putting an end to the bloody feud between Muslims and Hindus. How distant that fast of 1924 seemed.

The old man accordingly set out with his stick and walked from village to village – to wipe away people's tears, he said. He was seventy-five and enjoying a new lease of life. One day

In Wavell's opinion it was Jinnah, president of the Muslim League, who was to blame for the failure of the Simla conference (above, front-page headline of the *Sunday Amrita Bazar Patrika*, 15 July 1945). Congress was a national body representing all India's religions; the Muslim League was a religious organization. By demanding that all the Muslims elected to the viceroy's council should be from his League, Jinnah was excluding de facto the great number of Muslim members of Congress: it was the surest way to wreck the future of Indian unity.

Below: Gandhi with Lord Pethick-Lawrence, secretary of state for India (1945–7), who failed in his mission to try to make Hindus and Muslims understand each other. In Gandhi's eyes the partition of India into two nations was a 'blasphemy'. He wrote in *Harijan* that beyond the confines of the Muslim League there was abundant evidence to show the quasi-universal desire for Indian unity; but Gandhi was soon alone in dreaming of India's lost unity. His fellow campaigners were too impatient and partition was inevitable.

The two Indias, Hindu and Muslim (dating to the Mogul invasions), merged like the waters of a single river. (In 1987 there were 700 million Hindus and 70 million Muslims in India.) Each had its own architecture, as demonstrated by this Hindu temple (opposite) in Madurai, southern India, and the mosque (below) at Lucknow in northern India.

20032. P.Z.- LUCKNOW. MODJIBAMAN.

he would ask for food and lodging in a Muslim house, the next in a Hindu house; he asked Muslims and Hindus to undertake to protect one another's communities; he recited the Koran, the Bible and the Bhagavadgita. And he ignored the abuse and the insults, the excrement spread on the road and the bits of glass intended to cut his feet: he just kept on walking and praying and bringing people back together.

On 20 February 1947 Attlee had announced to the House of Commons that India's last viceroy, Louis Mountbatten (1900–79), would be quitting India by June 1948 and that India would henceforth be independent: this time a date had been fixed. In Delhi Lord Mountbatten had a lengthy interview with Gandhi, and then Jinnah, who successfully brandished the threat of civil war: as long as the country remained unified, he forecast, the bloody rioting would continue.

The die was cast and one night saw the rapid and bloody birth of two countries – Jinnah's Pakistan and Nehru's India. For Gandhi neither country was India

Gandhi was living in Banghi Colony in Delhi, the area where the Untouchables lived, and each evening he struggled to hold a prayer meeting, as he had in Noakhali and in Bihar. He was fighting against the odds: he was banned from publicly reciting the Koran; people called him 'Mohammed Gandhi'; they told him that rioting had started again in Bihar and he hurried to Bihar, only to find that people were killing each other in Noakhali. He tried to persuade Jinnah to accept the position of prime minister of a united India, but without success. No one, it seemed, was prepared to listen to him any more. Gandhi had never known defeat before, but now he was fighting with obscurity. Patel finally agreed to the principle of partition; then Nehru yielded, reluctantly: Congress was weary; after all the years of struggle the old campaigners had had enough. Mountbatten embarked on preparations for the partition of India: the Mahatma had lost.

He had a foreboding of problems in Calcutta and made his way there as fast as he could. Even now, he felt, it might still be possible to prove that the two communities could live together in harmony.

Nehru (above) giving his Independence Day speech (15 August 1948) at the illustrious Red Fort, a former Mogul stronghold in Delhi, where it is still given each year. In Gandhi's absence, it was Nehru who made the first Independence Day speech in 1947.

On 15 August 1947 the Indian flag was raised in place of the Union Jack. The colours of Congress – orange, white and green – bore Emperor Ashoka's wheel in place of Gandhi's spinning wheel. Speeches all through the night paid homage to 'the Father of the Nation' and crowds, drunk on freedom, shouted: 'Victory to Mahatma Gandhi!' The Mahatma himself called the day a 'spiritual tragedy' and spent it fasting.

Gandhi spent 15 August 1947 in Calcutta, refusing the honours extended to him. He did not deliver an official message. Instead he simply fasted.

The great exodus had begun. Twelve million refugees left their homes and villages and headed for a new country – Muslims abandoning India and crossing over into Pakistan, and Hindus, trapped in the new Muslim state, the 'country of the pure', crossing back into India.

CHAPTER 6
MARTYRDOM

As the refugees streamed between India and Pakistan hunger, panic, disease and the intense heat led to angry scenes and full-scale massacres. The Punjab was a battlefield before independence. Lahore, which was to become part of Pakistan, was put to fire and the sword. In Amritsar Hindus disguised as Muslims threw nitric acid in the eyes of Muslims in the bazaars.

Opposite: Muslim refugees, September 1947. Right: Muslim children in Pakistan, c. 1948.

Mountbatten stayed on as governor general, at Nehru's request, and armed a special task force of twenty-five thousand men – too few, as it soon transpired. On Independence Day itself a train full of corpses arrived at Amritsar station with 'Independence present for Nehru' scrawled in white letters on the final carriage.

Calcutta, however, was unaffected by the troubles. Young Hindu and Muslim women filed past the Mahatma to pay their respects; people made pilgrimages to see him and all day, while he continued with his spinning, he was surrounded by adoring crowds. Surhawardy, the leader of the Calcutta Muslims – who was in part responsible for the massacres – urged people to shout 'Long live India!' during Gandhi's public prayers. Despite his reticence and his personal suffering, Gandhi had succeeded in bringing calm to this most inflammable of cities, a city dedicated to the goddess of destruction.

It was not to last. At the end of August the troubles started. There was an attack on Gandhi's house. The attackers, who were after Surhawardy, hurled bricks; the police were called, and in the ensuing riot a number of people were killed. On 2 September Gandhi resolved to fast until Calcutta came to its senses.

Although he recoiled in horror and sadness from the vision that now confronted him, Gandhi still seemed to possess a magical ability to touch the heart of India. The first delegations arrived on 2 September itself, determined once again to save the Mahatma's life. Indian and even British policemen fasted in sympathy while continuing to carry out their duties. Hindus and Muslims filed past Gandhi's bedside, and even the murderers came to lay down their arms with tears in their eyes; but Gandhi was not yet satisfied. He wanted a written promise. On 4 September he received it; the riots had stopped for good in Calcutta, and he could now leave.

Opposite: scene of a confrontation between Muslims and Hindus in Delhi around the time of independence in 1947.

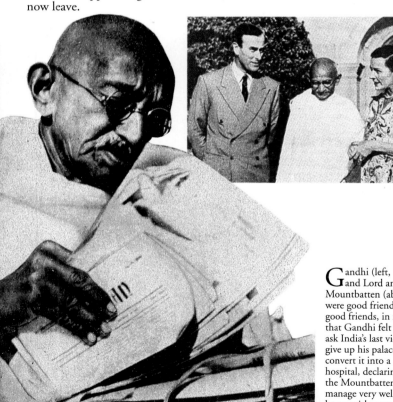

Gandhi (left, c. 1947) and Lord and Lady Mountbatten (above) were good friends – such good friends, in fact, that Gandhi felt able to ask India's last viceroy to give up his palace and convert it into a hospital, declaring that the Mountbattens could manage very well in a house without servants.

Thanks to Gandhi's efforts the troubles ceased in Calcutta. He moved on to Delhi, the capital and political heart of India, and began another fast in pursuit of national peace

In Delhi too there had been countless deaths. The Hindu and Sikh refugees from the Punjab had taken over Banghi Colony, the Untouchables' quarter, where Gandhi had once lived. He was obliged to move to Birla House, the home of a wealthy Hindu friend of long standing.

The day after his arrival Gandhi began visiting the refugee camps on his own, refusing to yield to requests that he take an armed escort, despite the obvious risk of assassination – either by Hindus opposed to his pro-Muslim tendencies or by Muslims on the grounds that he was a Hindu.

The 'senseless destruction', as Gandhi called it, continued. The epic birth of this country – whose freedom he had won by non-violent means – was marked by the most appalling scenes – children chopped in half, their heads smashed against walls, women thrown into wells by the hundreds. Hindus, Muslims and Sikhs were all responsible for the atrocities. As a Hindu himself, Gandhi was harshest in his criticism of the Hindus, and it was the hearts of Delhi's Muslims that he sought to appease by undertaking a new fast. In fact by now the rioting was almost over.

What the Mahatma wanted, however, was universal peace, and he had still not achieved his goal. Close to despair, he decided to fast again – for Hindu-Muslim

When he was no longer able to live in the Untouchables' quarter in Delhi, Gandhi accepted the hospitality of the wealthy Hindu Birla and lived in Birla's huge colonnaded villa (opposite), where he maintained his sober lifestyle.

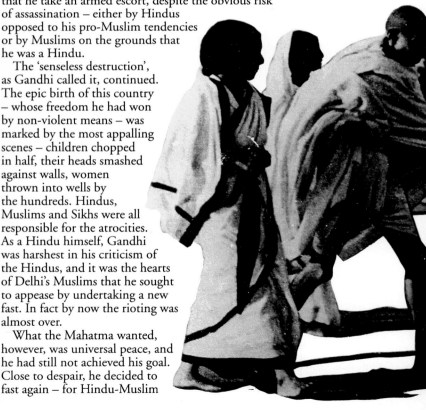

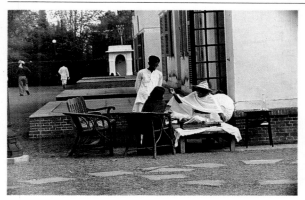

Gandhi (opposite, with members of his family) had an extraordinary relationship with children. He was enormously gentle and affectionate with them and throughout his life he adopted children spontaneously, including in 1918, a little Untouchable girl named Lakshmi who came to his ashram with her parents, and also the daughter of a British admiral. However, his eldest son, Harilal, regularly refused to have anything to do with him and ended his days destitute.

unity, but also as a means of healing himself. The fast began on 13 January 1948. Once again the delegations filed past his bed; once again he demanded written promises safeguarding the lives, property and religion of the Muslim people. On 18 January, in the presence of the Pakistani ambassador, he finally broke his fast.

Only two days later a bomb was thrown at Birla House during Gandhi's public prayer meeting. The would-be assassin, a Hindu by the name of Madan Lal, was arrested. He belonged to a small group of Hindu extremists who were determined to see Gandhi dead. They had been incited by one of the Mahatma's final demands – the payment of 550 million rupees due to Pakistan.

On 30 January Gandhi received a visit from Sardar Vallabhbhai Patel, deputy prime minister of the new government of India, that made him five minutes late for the start of his public prayer meeting. Annoyed at the delay, he left Birla House and crossed the garden, leaning on his two great-nieces, Abha and Manu.

The editor of the weekly pro-Hindu *Mahasabha*, Nathuram Godse, approached Gandhi and bent down to touch his feet as a sign of homage. Gandhi joined his hands together and smiled his famous 'toothless smile'. Suddenly Godse took out a small revolver and fired three shots, and Gandhi collapsed, murmuring the name of God.

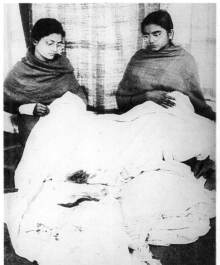

He died as he had wished, with the name of God, 'Hè Rama', on his lips. India and the rest of the world were in a state of shock. His funeral service was heroic, heartbreaking – a fitting tribute

Nehru rushed straight to Delhi, closely followed by Mountbatten. In a state of shock, Nehru made the official announcement – on All India Radio at 6 pm – that Mahatma Gandhi had been assassinated that afternoon by a Hindu. The army and the police were put on alert.

That night there was silence and a blackout across the whole of India. At dawn Gandhi's son Devadas and a group of Gandhi's disciples washed his body in the prescribed manner.

Gandhi's two great-nieces Abha and Manu (with Gandhi, opposite, in 1947) were his regular companions after Kasturbai's death. He had brought up the two orphans and shared a bed with Manu, his favourite, as a way of testing their virtue. The ensuing scandal was deeply mortifying to Gandhi. The two young women (above) hold his blood-stained shawl after his death in 1948.

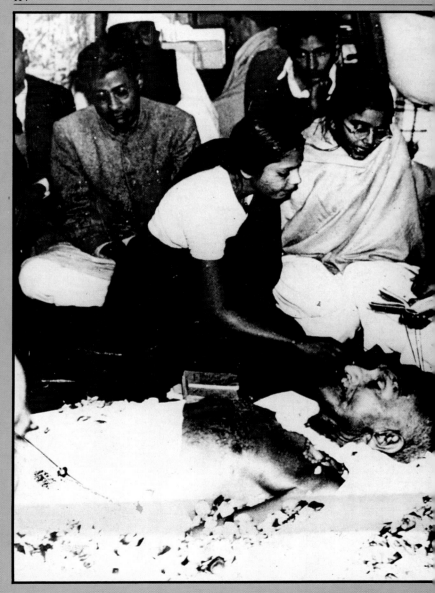

**'The Mahatma has been assassinated. His assassin is a Hindu'
(Lord Mountbatten)**

Nathuram Godse (above) belonged to a poor Brahman family that was fiercely traditionalist. He was stupid and maladjusted, incapable of holding down a steady job. In 1947 he was working as a tailor and was obsessed with politics. As a follower of Gandhi's he had spent some time in prison, but he had later come under the influence of a dangerous guru, Vir Sarvakar, an opium addict fanatically driven by the notion of Brahman superiority. During the trial that led to his hanging in 1949 Godse claimed full responsibility for murdering Gandhi (left, on his deathbed). He asked that his ashes be kept and scattered on the Indus only when India had been unified.

Subsequent pages: Gandhi's pyre (pp. 116–7); crowds watch as Gandhi's ashes are consigned to the Ganges and the Jumna (pp. 118–9).

The body was covered with roses and hoisted on to the roof of Birla House for a final *darshan* or meditation. Then the national flag was draped over the bier and the bier itself placed on the chassis of a Dodge 1500-weight weapon carrier pulled by two hundred soldiers. The Mahatma's cortege left at 11.45 am and arrived at the cremation site at 4.20 pm. Two million Indians stood by as the body burnt on its sandalwood pyre and the small man with his serene smile was lost for ever among the flames. At dawn next day relatives and close friends collected the ashes.

Over ten nights were due to pass before the ashes were scattered on the doubly sacred waters of India's two great rivers, the Ganges and the Jumna.

Now that he had gone, the question on everyone's lips was how he could have succeeded in liberating India in a single lifetime. Sanctified throughout India, Gandhi had achieved eternal status as the Father of the Nation. But was he no more than that?

Political leaders worldwide paid homage to him as though he were a head of state; but this was precisely what Gandhi was not and had never wanted to be: suddenly given the opportunity to govern, he retreated to a still higher plane. At the time of his death Gandhi owned next to nothing (sandals, glasses, a watch,

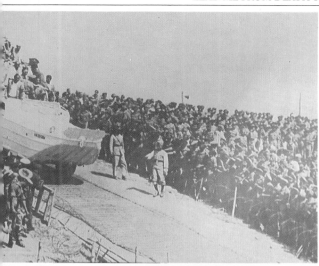

On the evening of Gandhi's death Nehru (opposite) addressed the whole of India on radio: 'The light has gone out of our lives and there is darkness everywhere and I do not quite know what to tell you and how to say it. Our beloved leader, Bapu, as we call him, the Father of our Nation, is no more. Perhaps I am wrong to say that. Nevertheless, we will not see him again as we have seen him these many years. We will not run to him for advice and seek solace from him, and that is a terrible blow not to me only but to millions and millions in this country. And it is difficult to soften the blow by any advice that I or anyone else can give you.

The light has gone out, I said, and yet I was wrong. For the light that shone in this country was no ordinary light ... and a thousand years later that light will still be seen in this country, and the world will see it.... For that light represented the living truth....'

Quoted in Louis Fischer
Life of Mahatma Gandhi, 1951

Gandhi's ashes are taken down to the river (top left), watched by a large crowd (left).

three little ivory monkeys and a handful of books), prompting comparisons with Buddha and Christ.

The comparisons were misleading. Gandhi was neither bigoted, fanatical, nor even especially devout, and nothing irritated him more than to be idolized by all those Indians who saw him as the incarnation of a new divinity. Unlike Buddha and Christ he was not seeking to reform the basis of his religion – not intent on turning moneylenders out of the temple. Nor was he what is known in India as a yogi, since the aim of the true yogi is complete detachment from the physical world through mental and physical exercises and a refusal to intervene in the course of events: Gandhi remained to the end firmly rooted in the world, exercising an influence on it through his actions.

While he was familiar with yoga practices, he was not a mystic. He was the first to admit that he had never experienced a state of ecstacy, in a country where it suffices to call yourself a saint for others to believe it.

Gandhi might in some respects be compared to Socrates. Socrates had his disciples and propounded philosophical principles – through dialogue and example – that disrupted the accepted order of things; but Socrates was not a revolutionary and he did not have an overwhelming impact on the history of Greece. There are still fewer parallels with Diogenes, for by renouncing material possessions and living in a tub Diogenes was turning his back on humanity rather than expressing his love for it.

Neither god, saint, mystic, sage, nor cynic, Gandhi eludes comparison, Western or Indian. Anchored in an ancient tradition that continued to evolve from day to day, he was nevertheless resolutely modern and the

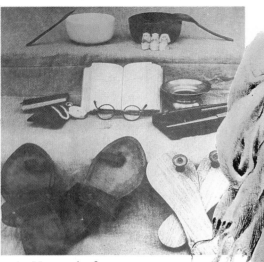

Gandhi's few belongings (below), including two pairs of sandals made in his ashram, a steel Ingersoll watch (stolen and later returned to him), eating utensils, his round-rimmed glasses, one of his holy books (the Bhagavadgita, the Koran and the Bible) and three little ivory monkeys – the first of which covers its ears, the second its eyes and the third its mouth – embodying the philosophy 'Hear no evil; see no evil; speak no evil'.

Gandhi (right) in 1930.

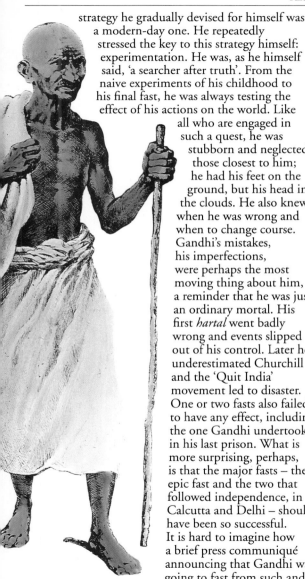

strategy he gradually devised for himself was a modern-day one. He repeatedly stressed the key to this strategy himself: experimentation. He was, as he himself said, 'a searcher after truth'. From the naive experiments of his childhood to his final fast, he was always testing the effect of his actions on the world. Like all who are engaged in such a quest, he was stubborn and neglected those closest to him; he had his feet on the ground, but his head in the clouds. He also knew when he was wrong and when to change course. Gandhi's mistakes, his imperfections, were perhaps the most moving thing about him, a reminder that he was just an ordinary mortal. His first *hartal* went badly wrong and events slipped out of his control. Later he underestimated Churchill and the 'Quit India' movement led to disaster. One or two fasts also failed to have any effect, including the one Gandhi undertook in his last prison. What is more surprising, perhaps, is that the major fasts – the epic fast and the two that followed independence, in Calcutta and Delhi – should have been so successful. It is hard to imagine how a brief press communiqué announcing that Gandhi was going to fast from such and

●People will write the life of Gandhi and they will discuss and criticize him and his theories and activities. But to some of us he will remain something apart from theory – a radiant and beloved figure who ennobled and gave some significance to our petty lives, and whose passing away has left us with a feeling of emptiness and loneliness. Many pictures rise in my mind of this man, whose eyes were often full of laughter and yet were proofs of infinite sadness. But the picture that is dominant and most significant is as I saw him marching, staff in hand, to Dandi on the salt march in 1930. Here was the pilgrim on his quest of Truth, quiet, peaceful, determined and fearless, who would continue that quest and pilgrimage, regardless of consequences.●

Jawaharlal Nehru
Foreword to
D. G. Tendulkar
Mahatma: Life of Mohandas Karamchand Gandhi, vol. 1, 1951

such a time could have been sufficient to reduce hardened killers to tears. Certainly Gandhi owed this success in part to the inspiration of his 'inner voice'; but it is also worth remembering that years of training had made him a past master of dramatic effects. He relied for his success on public opinion, and it was to public opinion that he had been appealing from his very first campaigns in South Africa. There could be nothing more democratic than Gandhi's methods: it was the people (*demos* in Greek) who judged him, who followed or refused to follow him, who rallied or hurled stones. British democracy had clearly served him well: Gandhi was fighting against Britain with its own weapons, snatched from its own democratic traditions.

To the question of whether he was mad or, in modern parlance, neurotic the answer is of course yes, to the extent that we all are – and, like all heroes, rather more

so. His neuroses and his aberrations were as public, however, as his victories, and it was Gandhi himself, in his autobiography, who exposed his obsession with cleanliness and hygiene and above all his interminable struggle with his own sexuality. In preference to the insular life of the family he opted for a monastic style of life in line with a Hindu tradition that cannot readily be understood according to Western criteria. He was certainly tyrannical, but most of all

'Death for me would be a glorious deliverance, rather than that I should be a helpless witness of the destruction of India, Hinduism, Sikhism and Islam.... I am in God's hands.'

Gandhi (during his last fast)
Quoted in
D. G. Tendulkar
Mahatma: Life of Mohandas Karamchand Gandhi, vol. 1, 1951

Photographs of Gandhi (centre) towards the end of his life and (below) with his entourage.

towards himself, constantly exercising his will in an effort to gain ever greater control of his body. In this area if he was 'a searcher', he was also an athlete, both mental and physical. His continuing struggle for freedom until the age of seventy-eight, his asceticism, his lengthy marches and extraordinary death-defying fasts are all a testimony to this fact. Most importantly he knew how to smile.

People who knew him describe Gandhi as a child and say that he laughed like a child. It is quite clear that throughout his life he was a profoundly cheerful person, intrinsically mischievous. In the course of time, however, this eternal child became more and more of a mother figure and the instinct that had prompted him as a child to bandage the mangoes on the trees in his parents' garden led him to care for his dying father, for his sick son, for Kasturbai, and for his favourite daughter – India – with the tender solicitude of a mother. Gandhi was the mother rather than 'father' of the nation.

He may have borrowed the concepts of civil disobedience and non-violence (this from Jainism), but

He is the One Luminous, Creator of All, Mahatma, Always in the hearts of the people enshrined, Revealed through Love, Intuition, and Thought, Whoever knows Him, Immortal becomes.

Quoted in D. G. Tendulkar, *Mahatma: Life of Mohandas Karamchand Gandhi* 8 vols, 1951–4

Below: popular image of Nehru and Gandhi, c. 1940.

the fast unto death was his own invention, the source in part of his greatness, and it remained inimitable, like his 'chivalry' – the way he spared his enemy once he was down, the way he gave a polite warning of a forthcoming conflict, the way he avoided burning his bridges, laying the groundwork for the future.

Each stage in the evolution from Gandhi the lawyer in his wing collar to Gandhi the little man in the loincloth and round-rimmed glasses corresponded to a psychological shift. Gandhi created an image that represented him in his totality, and that at the same time represented, as it were, the quintessence of India. This synthesis was made possible by his extraordinary mental energy: Gandhi was above all a mental athlete.

'I know no other man of any time or indeed in recent history who so forcefully and convincingly demonstrated the power of spirit over material things' (Sir Stafford Cripps)

On 11 February 1948, twelve days after the cremation, the urn containing Gandhi's ashes was taken by special train to Allahabad, at the confluence of the Ganges and the Jumna. A white boat carrying the prime minister of free India left the bank and Ramdas Gandhi tipped Gandhi's ashes into the waters of the two sacred rivers. Leaf boats full of flowers, fruit and milk floated alongside the ashes.

In June 1948 Lord Mountbatten left India.

During the summer Gandhi's eldest son Harilal – who had taken to calling himself Mohammed Gandhi – died in obscurity in a provincial hospital. He was an alcoholic and had been suffering from tuberculosis.

On 11 September of that same year Jinnah, governor general of Pakistan, died of cancer in Karachi. He had been aware for some time that he was terminally ill.

Meanwhile Nehru, whom Gandhi called the 'jewel of India', had shouldered a historic burden: the responsibility for a newly democratic India.

'Generations to come, it may be, will scarce believe that such a one as this ever in flesh and blood walked upon this earth.**'**
Albert Einstein in Louis Fischer (ed.), *The Essential Gandhi*, 1962

Overleaf: Gandhi in Noakali, c. 1947.

DOCUMENTS

'His smile is delightful, his laughter
infectious, and he radiates light-
heartedness. There is something childlike
about him which is full of charm.'
Jawaharlal Nehru
An Autobiography, 1991

The Benares scandal

6 February 1916: Gandhi (below) has now ended his year of political silence. He makes one of his first public speeches since returning from South Africa – at the inaugural ceremony of the new Hindu university in Benares, founded by Annie Besant. In attendance are Mrs Besant, numerous maharajahs and the viceroy.

Friends, I wish to tender my humble apology for the long delay that took place before I was able to reach this place. And you will readily accept the apology when I tell you that I am not responsible for the delay nor is any human agency responsible for it. *(Laughter.)* The fact is that I am like an animal on show and my keepers in their over-kindness always manage to neglect a necessary chapter in this life and that is pure accident. In this case, they did not provide for the series of accidents that happened to us – to me, my keepers, and my carriers. Hence this delay.

Friends, under the influence of the matchless eloquence of the lady (Mrs Besant) who has just sat down, pray, do not believe that our University has become a finished product and that all the young men who are to come to the University that has yet to rise and come into existence, have also come and returned from it finished citizens of a great empire. Do not go away with any such impression and if you, the student world to which my remarks are supposed to be addressed this evening, consider for one moment that the spiritual life, for which this country is noted and for which this country has no rival, can be transmitted through the lip, pray, believe me you are wrong. You will never be able merely through the lip to give the message that India, I hope, will one day deliver to the world. I myself have been 'fed up' with speeches and lectures. I except [sic] the lectures that have been delivered here during the last two days from this category, because they were necessary.

But I do venture to suggest to you that we have now reached almost the end of our resources in speech-making, and it is not enough that our ears are feasted, that our eyes are feasted, but it is necessary that our hearts have got to be touched and that our hands and feet have got to be moved. We have been told during the last two days how necessary it is, if we are to retain our hold upon the simplicity of Indian character, that our hands and feet should move in unison with our hearts. But this is only by way of preface. I wanted to say it is a matter of deep humiliation and shame for us that I am compelled this evening under the shadow of this great college, in this sacred city, to address my countrymen in a language that is foreign to me. I know that if I was appointed an examiner to examine all those who have been attending during these two days this series of lectures, most of those who might be examined upon these lectures would fail. And why? Because they have not been touched. I was present at the sessions of the great Congress in the month of December. There was a much vaster audience, and will you believe me when I tell you that the only speeches that touched that huge audience in Bombay were the speeches that were delivered in Hindustani? In Bombay, mind you, not in Benares where everybody speaks Hindi. But between the vernaculars of the Bombay Presidency on the one hand, and Hindi on the other, no such great dividing line exists as there does between English and the sister-languages of India; and the Congress audience was better able to follow the speakers in Hindi. I am hoping that this University will see to it that the youths who come to it will receive their instruction through the medium of their vernaculars. Our language is the reflection of ourselves, and if you tell me that our languages are too poor to express the best thought, then I say that the sooner we are wiped

out of existence, the better for us. Is there a man who dreams that English can ever become the national language of India? *(Cries of 'Never'.)* Why this handicap on the nation? Just consider for one moment what an unequal race our lads have to run with every English lad. I had the privilege of a close conversation with some Poona professors. They assured me that every Indian youth, because he reached his knowledge through the English language, lost at least six precious years of life. Multiply that by the number of students turned out by our schools and colleges and find out for yourselves how many thousand years have been lost to the nation. The charge against us is, that we have no initiative. How can we have any if we are to devote the precious years of our life to the mastery of a foreign tongue? We fail in this attempt also. Was it possible for any speaker yesterday and today to impress his audience as was possible for Mr Higginbotham? It was not the fault of the previous speakers that they could not engage the audience. They had more than substance enough for us in their addresses. But their addresses could not go home to us. I have heard it said that after all it is English-educated India which is leading and which is doing all the things for the nation. It would be monstrous if it were otherwise. The only education we receive is English education. Surely we must show something for it. But suppose that we had been receiving during the past fifty years education through our vernaculars, what should we have had today? We should have today a free India, we should have our educated men, not as if they were foreigners in their own land but speaking to the heart of the nation; they would be working amongst the poorest of the poor, and whatever they would have gained during the past 50 years would be a heritage for the nation. *(Applause.)* Today even our wives are not the sharers in our best thought. Look at Professor Bose [a botanist] and Professor Ray [a chemist] and their brilliant researches. Is it not a shame that their researches are not the common property of the masses?

Let us now turn to another subject.

The Congress has passed a resolution about self-government and I have no doubt that the All-India Congress Committee and the Moslem League will do their duty and come forward with some tangible suggestions. But I, for one, must frankly confess that I am not so much interested in what they will be able to produce as I am interested in anything that the student world is going to produce or the masses are going to produce. No paper contribution will ever give us self-government. No amount of speeches will ever make us fit for self-government. It is only our conduct that will fit us for it. *(Applause.)* And how are we trying to govern ourselves? I want to think audibly this evening. I do not want to make a speech and if you find me this evening speaking without reserve, pray, consider that you are only sharing the thoughts of a man who allows himself to think audibly, and if you think that I seem to transgress the limits that courtesy imposes upon me, pardon me for the liberty I may be taking. I visited the Viswanath Temple last evening and as I was walking through those lanes, these were the thoughts that touched me. If a stranger dropped from above on to this great temple and he had to consider what we as Hindus were, would he not be justified in condemning us? Is not this great temple a reflection of our own character? I speak feelingly as a Hindu.

Is it right that the lanes of our sacred temple should be as dirty as they are? The houses round about are built anyhow. The lanes are tortuous and narrow. If even our temples are not models of roominess and cleanliness, what can our self-government be? Shall our temples be abodes of holiness, cleanliness and peace as soon as the English have retired from India, either of their own pleasure or by compulsion, bag and baggage?

I entirely agree with the President of the Congress that before we think of self-government, we shall have to do the necessary plodding. In every city there are two divisions, the cantonment and the city proper. The city mostly is a stinking den. But we are a people unused to city life. But if we want city life, we cannot reproduce the easy-going hamlet life. It is not comforting to think that people walk about the streets of Indian Bombay under the perpetual fear of dwellers in the storeyed buildings spitting upon them. I do a great deal of railway travelling. I observe the difficulty of third-class passengers. But the Railway Administration is by no means to blame for all their hard lot. We do not know the elementary laws of cleanliness. We spit anywhere on the carriage floor, irrespective of the thought that it is often used as sleeping space. We do not trouble ourselves as to how we use it; the result is indescribable filth in the compartment. The so-called better class passengers over-awe their less fortunate brethren. Among them I have seen the student world also. Sometimes they behave no better. They can speak English and they have worn Norfolk Jackets and therefore claim the right to force their way in and command seating accommodation. I have turned the searchlight all over and as you have given me the privilege of speaking to you, I am laying my heart bare. Surely we must set these things right in our progress towards self-government. I now introduce you to another scene. His Highness the Maharajah, who presided yesterday over our deliberations, spoke about the poverty of India. Other speakers laid great stress upon it. But what did we witness in the great *pandal* in which the foundation ceremony was performed by the viceroy? Certainly a most gorgeous show, an exhibition of jewellery which made a splendid feast for the eyes of the greatest jeweller who chose to come from Paris. I compare with the richly bedecked noblemen the millions of the poor. And I feel like saying to these noblemen: 'There is no salvation for India unless you strip yourselves of this jewellery and hold it in trust for your countrymen in India.' *('Hear, hear' and applause.)* I am sure it is not the desire of the King-Emperor or Lord Hardinge that in order to show the truest loyalty to our King-Emperor, it is necessary for us to ransack our jewellery-boxes and to appear bedecked from top to toe. I would undertake at the peril of my life to bring to you a message from King George himself that he expects nothing of the kind. Sir, whenever I hear of a great palace rising in any great city of India, be it in British India or be

it in India which is ruled by our great chiefs, I become jealous at once and I say: 'Oh, it is the money that has come from the agriculturists.' Over seventy-five per cent of the population are agriculturists and Mr Higginbotham told us last night in his own felicitous language that they are the men who grow two blades of grass in the place of one. But there cannot be much spirit of self-government about us if we take away or allow others to take away from them almost the whole of the results of their labour. Our salvation can only come through the farmer. Neither the lawyers, nor the doctors, nor the rich landlords are going to secure it.

Now, last but not the least, it is my bounden duty to refer to what agitated our minds during these two or three days. All of us have had many anxious moments while the viceroy was going through the streets of Benares. There were detectives stationed in many places. We were horrified. We asked ourselves: 'Why this distrust? Is it not better that even Lord Hardinge should die than live a living death?' But a representative of a mighty Sovereign may not. He might find it necessary even to live a living death. But why was it necessary to impose these detectives on us? We may foam, we may fret, we may resent but let us not forget that India of today in her impatience has produced an army of anarchists. I myself am an anarchist, but of another type. But there is a class of anarchists amongst us, and if I was able to reach this class, I would say to them that their anarchism has no room in India if India is to conquer the conqueror. It is a sign of fear. If we trust and fear God, we shall have to fear no one, not maharajahs, not viceroys, not the detectives, not even King George. I honour the anarchist for his love of the

The Ghats, at Benares, c. 1920. Previous page: maharajahs in London, 1930.

country. I honour him for his bravery in being willing to die for his country; but I ask him: Is killing honourable? Is the dagger of an assassin a fit precursor of an honourable death? I deny it. There is no warrant for such methods in any scriptures. If I found it necessary for the salvation of India that the English should retire, that they should be driven out, I would not hesitate to declare that they would have to go, and I hope I would be prepared to die in defence of that belief. That would, in my opinion, be an honourable death. The bomb-thrower creates secret plots, is afraid to come into the open, and when caught pays the penalty of misdirected zeal. I have been told: 'Had we not done this, had some people not thrown bombs, we should never have gained what we have got with reference to the partition movement.' *(Mrs Besant: 'Please stop it.')*

This was what I said in Bengal when Mr Lyons presided at the meeting. I think what I am saying is necessary. If I am told to stop, I shall obey. *(Turning to the Chairman)* I await your orders. If you consider that by my speaking as I am, I am not serving the country and the Empire, I shall certainly stop. *(Cries of 'Go on'.) (The Chairman: 'Please explain your object.')* I am explaining my object. I am simply *(Another interruption)*. My friends, please do not resent this interruption. If Mrs Besant this evening suggests that I should stop, she does so because she loves India so well, and she considers that I am erring in thinking audibly before you young men. But even so, I simply say this that I want to purge India of the atmosphere of suspicion on either side; if we are to reach our goal, we should have an empire which is to be based upon mutual love and mutual trust. Is it not better that we talk under the shadow of this college than that we should be talking irresponsibly in our homes? I consider that it is much better that we talk [about] these things openly. I have done so with excellent results before now. I know that there is nothing that the students are not discussing. There is nothing that the students do not know. I am therefore turning the searchlight towards ourselves. I hold the name of my country so dear to me that I exchange these thoughts with you and submit to you that there is no reason for anarchism in India. Let us frankly and openly say whatever we want to say to our rulers and face the consequences if what we have to say does not please them. But let us not abuse. I was talking the other day to a member of the much-abused civil service. I have not very much in common with the members of that service, but I could not help admiring the manner in which he was speaking to me. He said: 'Mr Gandhi, do you for one moment suppose that all we, civil servants, are a bad lot, that we want to oppress the people whom we have come to govern?' 'No,' I said. 'Then, if you get an opportunity, put in a word for the much-abused civil service.' And I am here to put in that word. Yes, many members of the Indian civil service are most decidedly overbearing, they are tyrannical, at times thoughtless. Many other adjectives may be used. I grant all these things and I grant also that after having lived in India for a certain number of years, some of them become somewhat degraded. But what does that signify? They were gentlemen before they came here, and if they have lost some of the moral fibre, it is a reflection upon ourselves. *(Cries of 'No'.)* Just think out for yourselves, if a man who was good yesterday has become bad after having come in contact with me, is he responsible that he has deteriorated or am I? The atmosphere of sycophancy and falsity that surrounds them on their coming to India demoralises them as it would many of us. It is well to take the blame sometimes. If we are to receive self-government, we shall have to take it. We shall never be granted self-government. Look at the history of the British Empire and the British nation; freedom-loving as it is, it will not be a party to give freedom to a people who will not take it themselves. Learn your lesson if you wish to from the Boer War. Those who were enemies of that Empire only a few years ago have now become friends.

(At this point there was an interruption and there was a movement on the platform to leave; the speech therefore ended here abruptly.)

The Collected Works of Mahatma Gandhi, vol. 13, 1964

The rules of the *satyagrahasrama*

Gandhi was an enthusiastic advocate of community life. His ashrams – Phoenix, Tolstoy Farm, Sabarmati, Sevagram – were run with an emphasis on hygiene, politics and spirituality.

Gandhi leaves Sevagram (c. 1938) wearing his favourite headgear – a damp towel.

OBJECT
The object of the Ashram is to learn how to serve the motherland one's whole life and to serve it.

CLASSES
The Ashram consists of three classes: Controllers, Novitiates and Students.

(1) CONTROLLERS
The Controllers believe that, in order to learn how to serve the country, the following observances should be enforced in their own lives and they have been trying to do so for some time.

1. Vow of truth
It is not enough for a person under this vow that he does not ordinarily resort to untruth; such a person ought to know that no deception may be practised even for the good of the country. One should consider the example of Prahlad in order to understand how one should behave towards elders such as parents in the interests of Truth.

2. Vow of non-violence
It is not enough to refrain from taking the life of any living being. He who has pledged himself to this vow may not kill even those whom he believes to be unjust; he may not be angry with them, he must love them; thus, he would oppose the tyranny whether of parents, governments or others, but will never kill or hurt the tyrant. The follower of truth and non-violence will offer satyagraha against tyranny and win over the tyrant by love; he will not carry out the tyrant's will but he will suffer punishment even unto death for disobeying his will until the tyrant himself is won over.

3. Vow of celibacy
It is well-nigh impossible to observe

these two vows unless celibacy too is observed; and for this vow it is not enough that one does not look upon another woman with a lustful eye, one has so to control the animal passions that they will not be moved even in thought; if one is married, one will not have sexual intercourse even with one's wife, but, regarding her as a friend, will establish with her a relationship of perfect purity.

4. Control of the palate

Until one has overcome the palate, it is difficult to observe the foregoing vows, more especially that of celibacy. Control of the palate should therefore be treated as a separate observance by one desirous of serving the country and, believing that eating is only for sustaining the body, one should regulate and purify one's diet day by day. Such a person will immediately, or gradually, as he can, leave off such articles of food as may tend to stimulate animal passions.

5. Vow of non-stealing

It is not enough not to steal what is commonly considered as other men's property. One who has pledged himself to this vow should realize that Nature provides from day to day just enough and no more for one's daily needs by way of food and so hold it theft to use articles of food, dress, etc, which one does not really need and live accordingly.

6. Vow of non-possession

It is not enough not to possess and keep much, but it is necessary not to keep anything which may not be absolutely necessary for the nourishment and protection of our body: thus, if one can do without chairs, one should do so. He who has taken this vow will always bear

this in mind and endeavour to simplify his life more and more.

SUBSIDIARY OBSERVANCES

1. Vow of Swadeshi

The person who has taken the vow of Swadeshi will never use articles which conceivably involve violation of truth in their manufacture or on the part of their manufacturers. It follows, for instance, that a votary of truth will not use articles manufactured in the mills of Manchester, Germany or India, for he cannot be sure that they involve no such violation of truth. Moreover, labourers suffer much in the mills. The generation of tremendous heat causes enormous destruction of life. Besides, the loss of workers' lives in the manufacture of machines and of other creatures through excessive heat is something impossible to describe. Foreign cloth and cloth made by means of machinery are, therefore, tabooed to a votary of non-violence as they involve triple violence. Further reflection will show that the use of foreign cloth can be held to involve a breach of the vows of non-stealing and non-possession. We follow custom and, for better appearance, wear foreign cloth in preference to the cloth made on our own handlooms with so little effort. Artificial beautifying of the body is a hindrance to a *brahmachari* and so, even from the point of view of that vow, machine-made cloth is taboo. Therefore, the vow of Swadeshi requires the use of simple clothing made on simple handlooms and stitched in simple style, foreign buttons, cuts, etc, being avoided. The same line of reasoning may be applied to all other articles.

2. Vow of fearlessness

He who is acted upon by fear can hardly observe the vows of truth, etc.

The Controllers will, therefore, constantly endeavour to be free from the fear of kings or society, one's caste or family, thieves, robbers, ferocious animals such as tigers, and even of death. One who observes the vow of fearlessness will defend himself or others by truth-force or soul-force.

3. Vow against untouchability

According to Hindu religion as traditionally practised, communities such as *Dhed*, *Bhangi*, etc, known by the names of *Antyaj*, *Pancham*, *Achhut* and so on, are looked upon as untouchable. Hindus belonging to other communities believe that they will be defiled if they touch a member of any of the said communities and, if anyone does so accidentally, he thinks that he has committed a sin. The founders of the Ashram believe that this practice is a blot on Hindu religion. Themselves staunch Hindus, they believe that the Hindu race will continue to add to its load of sin so long as it regards a single community as untouchable. Some of the consequences of this practice have been terrible. In order to be free from this sin, the Ashram inmates are under a vow to regard the untouchable communities as touchable; actually one *Dhed* family was staying in the Ashram, and it is still there, when the third edition of these rules was being drawn up. It lives exactly in the same condition as others in the Ashram do. This vow does not extend to association for purpose of eating. All that is desired is the eradication of the evil of untouchability.

Varnashram

The Ashram does not follow the *varnashram* [the organisation of society into four castes, each with a distinctive function, and the division of life into four stages] dharma. Where those in control of the Ashram will take the place of the pupils' parents and where life-long vows of celibacy, non-hoarding, etc, are to be observed, *varnashram* dharma has no scope. The Ashram inmates will be in the stage of *sanyasis* [those who, in the last stage of life, have renounced the world] and so it is not necessary for them to follow the rules of this dharma. Apart from this, the Ashram has a firm belief in the *varnashram* dharma. The discipline of caste seems to have done no harm to the country; on the contrary, rather. There is no reason to believe that eating in company promotes brotherhood ever so slightly. In order that the *varnashram* dharma and caste discipline might in no way be undermined, the Ashram inmates are under obligation, whenever they stir out, to subsist on fruits if they cannot cook their own food.

MOTHER TONGUE

It is the belief of the Controllers that no nation or any group thereof can make real progress by abandoning its own language; they will, therefore, use their own language. As they desire to be on terms of intimacy with their brethren from all parts of India, they will also learn the chief Indian languages; as Sanskrit is a key to Indian languages, they will learn that too.

MANUAL WORK

The Controllers believe that body labour is a duty imposed by nature upon mankind. Such labour is the only means by which man may sustain himself; his mental and spiritual powers should be used for the common good only. As the vast majority in the world live on agriculture, the Controllers will always devote some part of their time to working on the land; when that is not possible, they will perform some other bodily labour.

WEAVING

The Controllers believe that one of the chief causes of poverty in the land is the virtual disappearance of spinning-wheels and handlooms. They will, therefore, make every effort to revive this industry by themselves weaving cloth on handlooms.

POLITICS

Politics, economic progress, etc, are not unconnected matters; knowing that they are all rooted in religion, the Controllers will make an effort to learn and teach politics, economics, social reform, etc, in a religious spirit and work in these fields with all the zeal that they can command.

(2) NOVITIATES

Those who are desirous of following the foregoing programme but are not able immediately to take the necessary vows may be admitted as Novitiates. It is obligatory upon them to conform to all the observances which are followed by Controllers the while that they are in the Ashram. They will acquire the status of Controllers when they are able to take the necessary vows for life.

(3) STUDENTS

1 Boys and girls under twelve years of age will not be admitted if their parents do not join at the same time.
2 Parents will have to surrender all control over their children.
3 Children will not be permitted to visit their parents for any reason until the whole course of study is finished.
4 Students will be taught to observe all the vows intended for the Controllers.
5 They will receive instruction in religion, agriculture, handloom-weaving and letters.

6 Instruction in letters will be through the students' own languages and will include History, Geography, Arithmetic, Algebra, Geometry, Economics, etc, the learning of Sanskrit, Hindi and at least one Dravidian language being obligatory.
7 English will be taught as a second language.
8 Urdu, Bengali, Tamil, Telugu, Devnagari and Gujarati scripts will be taught to all.
9 Upon reaching the age of majority, students will be given the option of taking the vows or retiring from the Ashram. This will make it possible for those to whom the programme has not commended itself to leave the Ashram.
10 They will exercise this option at any age when they will require no assistance from their parents or guardians.
11 Every endeavour will be made from the very beginning to see that, when they leave, they will be strong enough to have no fear what they would do for their maintenance.
12 Grown-up persons also may be admitted as students.
13 As a rule, everyone will wear the simplest and a uniform style of dress.
14 Food will be simple. Chillies will be excluded altogether and generally no condiments will be used excepting salt, pepper and turmeric. Milk, ghee and other milk products being a hindrance to a celibate life and milk being often a cause of tuberculosis and having the same stimulating qualities as meat, they will be most sparingly used, if at all. Meals will be served thrice a day and will include dried and fresh fruits in liberal quantities. All inmates of the Ashram will be taught the general principles of hygiene.

15 No holidays will be observed in this Ashram but, for one and a half days every week, the ordinary routine will be altered and everyone will have some time to attend to his private work.

16 During three months in the year, those whose health permits it will be taken on a tour, on foot for the most part, of India.

17 Nothing will be charged either from Students or Novitiates towards their monthly expenditure, but parents or the members themselves will be expected to contribute whatever they can towards the expenses of the Ashram.

MISCELLANEOUS

Administration of the Ashram will rest with a body of Controllers. The Chief Controller will have the right to decide whom to admit and to which category.

The expenses of the Ashram are being met from moneys already received by the Chief Controller or to be received from friends who may have some faith in the Ashram.

The Ashram is accommodated in two houses on the banks of the Sabarmati, Ahmedabad, on the road to Sarakhej across the Ellis Bridge.

It is expected that in a few months, about 250 acres of land will be acquired in the vicinity of Ahmedabad and the Ashram located thereon.

A REQUEST

Visitors are requested to observe all the Ashram rules during their stay there. Every endeavour will be made to make them comfortable; but the management will be thankful to them if they bring with them their bedding and utensils for meals, as the Ashram rules permit the stocking of only a minimum of articles.

Those parents who intend sending their children to the Ashram are advised

The Sabarmati ashram.

The Tolstoy Farm ashram.

to pay a visit to the Ashram. No boy or girl will be admitted before he or she has been duly tested.

DAILY ROUTINE

1) An effort is being made to see that everyone in the Ashram gets up at 4 o'clock. The first bell rings at 4.

(2) It is obligatory on all, except those who are ill, to get up at 4.30. Everyone finishes bathing by 5.

(3) 5 to 5.30: Prayers and readings from holy books.

(4) 5.30 to 7: Breakfast of fruits, such as bananas.

(5) 7 to 8.30. Manual work. This includes drawing water, grinding, sweeping, weaving, cooking, etc.

(6) 8.30 to 10: School work.

(7) 10 to 12: Meal and cleaning of utensils. The meal consists of dal, rice, vegetables and *rotlis* for five days. On two days, there are *rotlis* and fruits.

(8) 12 to 3: School work.

(9) 3 to 5: Work, as in the morning.

(10) 5 to 6: Meal and cleaning of utensils. The meal mostly follows the same pattern as in the morning.

(11) 6.30 to 7: Prayers, as in the morning.

(12) 7 to 9: Study, receiving visitors, etc. Before nine, all children go to bed. At ten the lights are put out.

For school work, the subjects of study at present are Sanskrit, Gujarati, Tamil, Hindi and Arithmetic. Study of History and Geography is included in that of languages.

No paid teachers or servants are employed in the Ashram.

The Collected Works of Mahatma Gandhi, vol. 13, 1964

The pledge

Gandhi addresses a rally on 11 September 1906 in Johannesburg. The Transvaal government obliged all Indians in South Africa (opposite) to have their fingerprints taken by the authorities; Indians pledge to defy the 'Black Law' and a new movement is born: satyagraha *(firmness in truth).*

Gandhi (c. 1912) with a fellow *satyagrahi*.

We all believe in one and the same God, the differences in nomenclature in Hinduism and Islam notwithstanding. To pledge ourselves or to take an oath in the name of that God or with Him as witness is not something to be trifled with. If having taken such an oath we violate our pledge we are guilty before God and man. Personally I hold that a man who deliberately and intelligently takes a pledge and then breaks it forfeits his manhood....

I know that pledges and vows are, and should be, taken on rare occasions.... But if I can imagine a crisis in the history of the Indian community of South Africa when it would be in the fitness of things to take pledges, that crisis is surely now.... The Government has taken leave of all sense of decency. We would only be betraying our unworthiness and cowardice, if we cannot stake our all in the face of the conflagration which envelopes [sic] us and sit watching it with folded hands. There is no doubt, therefore, that the present is a proper occasion for taking pledges. But every one of us must think out for himself if he has the will and the ability to pledge himself. Resolutions of this nature cannot be passed by a majority vote. Only those who take a pledge can be bound by it. This pledge must not be taken with a view to producing an effect on outsiders. No one should trouble to consider what impression it might have upon the Local Government, the Imperial Government, or the Government of India. Everyone must only search his own heart, and if the inner voice assures him that he has the requisite strength to carry him through, then only should he pledge himself and then only will his pledge bear fruit.... Therefore I want to give you an idea of the worst that might

happen to us in the present struggle.... We may have to go to jail, where we may be insulted. We may have to go hungry and suffer extreme heat or cold. Hard labour may be imposed upon us. We may be flogged by rude warders. We may be fined heavily and our property may be attached and held up to auction if there are only a few resisters left. Opulent today, we may be reduced to abject poverty tomorrow. We may be deported. Suffering from starvation and similar hardships in jail, some of us may fall ill and even die. In short, therefore, it is not at all impossible that we may have to endure every hardship that we can imagine....

A word about my personal responsibility. If I am warning you of the risks attendant upon the pledge, I am at the same time inviting you to pledge yourselves, and I am fully conscious of my responsibility in the matter. It is possible that a majority of those present here may take the pledge in a fit of enthusiasm or indignation but may weaken under the ordeal, and only a handful may be left to face the final test. Even then there is only one course open to someone like me, to die but not to submit to the law. It is quite unlikely but even if everyone else flinched leaving me alone to face the music, I am confident that I would never violate my pledge. Please do not misunderstand me. I am not saying this out of vanity, but I wish to put you, especially the leaders upon the platform, on your guard. I wish respectfully to suggest it to you that if you have not the will or the ability to stand firm even when you are perfectly isolated, you must not only not take the pledge yourselves but you must declare your opposition before the resolution is put to the meeting and before its members begin to take pledges and you must not make yourselves parties to the resolution. Although we are going to take the pledge in a body, no one should imagine that default on the part of one or many can absolve the rest from their obligation. Everyone should fully realize his responsibility, then only pledge himself independently of others and understand that he himself must be true to his pledge even unto death, no matter what others do.

The Collected Works of Mahatma Gandhi, vol. 29, 1968

What to do if you want to fast properly

Gandhi carried out many experiments in the pursuit of knowledge. After trying numerous ways of fasting he drew up these guidelines in 1925 for a successful fast – a cure for constipation, depression and an excess of high spirits.

From a layman's and from a purely physical standpoint I should lay down the following rules for all those who may wish to fast on any account whatsoever.

1. Conserve your energy both physical and mental from the very beginning.

2. You must cease to think of food whilst you are fasting.

3. Drink as much cold water as you can, with or without soda and salt, but in small quantities at a time (water should be boiled, strained and cooled). Do not be afraid of salt and soda, because most waters contain both these salts in a free state.

4. Have a warm sponge daily.

5. Take an enema regularly during fast. You will be surprised at the impurities you will expel daily.

Photograph taken during Gandhi's last fast, in 1948.

6. Sleep as much as possible in the open air.

7. Bathe in the morning sun. A sun and air bath is at least as great a purifier as a water bath.

8. Think of anything else but the fast.

9. No matter from what motive you are fasting, during this precious time, think of your Maker, and of your relation to Him and His other creation, and you will make discoveries you may not have even dreamed of.

With apologies to medical friends, but out of the fulness [sic] of my own experience and that of fellow-cranks I say without hesitation, fast (1) if you are constipated, (2) if you are anaemic, (3) if you are feverish, (4) if you have indigestion, (5) if you have a head-ache, (6) if you are rheumatic, (7) if you are gouty, (8) if you are fretting and foaming, (9) if you are depressed, (10) if you are over-joyed; and you will avoid medical prescriptions and patent medicines.

Eat *only* when you are *hungry* and when you have laboured for your food.

Gandhi
Young India 1924–6, 1927

Gandhi bathing at Cap Comorin.

A paradox

Gandhi (below) often shocked people, including his Jewish friends, when he urged them to pray for Hitler. Nehru used to be perplexed by him, but came to regard him as a 'philosophical anarchist', whose mind worked differently from other people's.

After the publication of this article in Harijan *on 11 November 1938, the Nazi press launched a fierce attack against Gandhi. Jews themselves were shocked by it and Gandhi's old friend Herman Kallenbach vehemently rejected the idea of 'praying for Hitler'. In 1946 Louis Fischer, author of a biography of the Mahatma, questioned him about the article. 'Hitler killed five million Jews,' Gandhi replied. 'It is the greatest crime of our time. But the Jews should have offered themselves to the butcher's knife. They should have thrown themselves into the sea from cliffs.... It would have aroused the world and the people of Germany.... As it is they succumbed anyway in their millions.'*

My sympathies are all with the Jews. They have been the untouchables of Christianity.... A Jewish friend has sent me a book called *The Jewish Contribution to Civilization*, by Cecil Roth. It gives a record of what the Jews have done to enrich the world's literature, art, music, drama, science, medicine, agriculture, etc ... the German persecution of the Jews seems to have no parallel in history. The tyrants of old never went so mad as Hitler seems to have done. If there ever could be a justifiable war in the name of and for humanity, war against Germany to prevent the wanton persecution of a whole race would be completely justified. But I do not believe in any war....

Can the Jews resist this organized and shameless persecution?... If I were a Jew and were born in Germany and earned my livelihood there, I would claim Germany as my home even as the tallest gentile German might, and challenge him to shoot me or cast me in the dungeon.... And for doing this

I should not wait for the fellow Jews to join me in civil resistance, but would have confidence that in the end the rest were bound to follow my example. If one Jew or all the Jews were to accept the prescription here offered, he or they cannot be worse off than now.... The calculated violence of Hitler may even result in a general massacre of the Jews by way of his first answer to the declaration of such hostilities. But if the Jewish mind could be prepared for voluntary sacrifice, even the massacre I have imagined could be turned into a day of thanksgiving that Jehovah had wrought deliverance of the race even at the hands of a tyrant. For to the God-fearing, death has no terror....

The Jews of Germany can offer Satyagraha under infinitely better auspices than the Indians of South Africa. The Jews are a compact, homogeneous community in Germany. They are far more gifted than the Indians of South Africa. And they have organized world opinion behind them. I am convinced that if someone with courage and vision can arise among them to lead them in non-violent action, the winter of their despair can in the twinkling of an eye be turned into the summer of hope. And what has today become a degrading man hunt can be turned into a calm and determined stand offered by unarmed men and women possessing the strength of suffering given to them by Jehovah.... The German Jews will score a lasting victory over the German gentiles in the sense that they will have converted the latter to an appreciation of human dignity.

Quoted in Louis Fischer, *The Life of Mahatma Gandhi*, 1951

Nehru and Gandhi.

'A philosophical anarchist'

He is an extraordinary paradox. I suppose all outstanding men are so to some extent. For years I have puzzled over this problem: why with all his love and solicitude for the under-dog he yet supports a system which inevitably produces it and crushes it; why with all his passion for non-violence he is in favour of a political and social structure which is wholly based on violence and coercion? Perhaps it is not correct to say that he is in favour of such a system; he is more or less of a philosophical anarchist. But as the ideal anarchist state is too far off still and cannot easily be conceived, he accepts the present order. It is not I think a question of means, that he objects, as he does, to the use of violence in bringing about a change. Quite apart from the methods to be adopted for changing the existing order, an ideal objective can be envisaged, something that is possible of achievement in the not distant future.

Jawaharlal Nehru
An Autobiography,
abridged by C. D. Narasimhaiah, 1991

15 August 1947

Gandhi (opposite) was economical not only with food, money and clothing but also with his voice. In preference to speaking he would often scribble notes on scraps of paper with a pencil stub. He chose to spend 15 August 1947 praying in Calcutta instead of taking advantage of the lavish honours that would have marked his attendance at the celebrations in Delhi. This is what he was doing on India's first day of independence.

Letter to Agatha Harrison

My dear Agatha,

This letter I am dictating whilst I am spinning. You know, my way of celebrating great events, such as today's, is to thank God for it and, therefore, to pray. This prayer must be accompanied by a fast, if the taking of fruit juices may be so described. And then as a mark of identification with the poor and dedication there must be spinning. Hence I must not be satisfied with the spinning I do every day, but I must do as much as is possible in consistence with my other appointments....
Love.

Bapu

Letter to Ramendra G. Sinha

Dear Friend,

I must take you at your word. As you say, your father had in him non-violence of the brave. Such a one never dies, destruction of the body has no meaning for him. Therefore, it is not right for you, your mother [or anyone] to mourn over the death of your brave father. He has left, in dying, a rich legacy which I hope you will all deserve. The best advice I can give is that you should all do whatever you can for the building up of the freedom that has come to us today and the first thing you can do is to copy your father's bravery.

Bravery of non-violence is shown in a variety of ways, not necessarily in dying at the hands of an assassin. There is no doubt that if you earn an honest price for the [loss] of your [dear ones] that by itself will be a contribution to the preservation of the [dearly earned freedom].
Yours sincerely,

M. K. Gandhi

[*The material in square brackets is illegible in the original.*]

Advice to West Bengal ministers

From today you have to wear the crown of thorns. Strive ceaselessly to cultivate truth and non-violence. Be humble. Be forbearing. The British rule no doubt put you on your mettle. But now you will be tested through and through. Beware of power; power corrupts. Do not let yourselves be entrapped by its pomp and pageantry. Remember, you are in office to serve the poor in India's villages. May God help you.

Talk with C. Rajagopalachari

The new Governor of the province, C. Rajagopalachari, paid him a respectful visit and congratulated him on the 'miracle which he had wrought'. But Gandhiji replied that he could not be satisfied until Hindus and Muslims felt safe in one another's company and returned to their own homes to live as before. Without that change of heart, there was likelihood of future deterioration in spite of the present enthusiasm.

Talk with Communist Party members

At 2, there was an interview with some members of the Communist Party of India to whom Gandhiji said that political workers, whether Communist or Socialist, must forget today all differences and help to consolidate the freedom which had been attained. Should we allow it to break into pieces? The tragedy was that the strength with which the country had fought against the British was failing them when it came to the establishment of Hindu-Muslim unity.

With regard to the celebrations, Gandhiji said: 'I can't afford to take part in this rejoicing, which is a sorry affair.'

Talk to students

Gandhiji explained in detail why the fighting must stop now. We had two States now, each of which was to have both Hindu and Muslim citizens. If that were so, it meant an end of the two-nation theory. Students ought to think and think well. They should do no wrong. It was wrong to molest an Indian citizen merely because he professed a different religion. Students should do everything to build up a new State of India which would be everybody's pride. With regard to the demonstration of fraternization he said: 'I am not lifted off my feet by these demonstrations of joy.'

The Collected Works of Mahatma Gandhi, vol. 89, 1983

An adopted daughter

The daughter of a British admiral, Madeleine Slade got to know Gandhi through the writer Romain Rolland and became one of his closest companions. Gandhi called her Mira after a 16th-century Rajput poet who steadfastly resisted the advances of her husband, dedicating her life to Krishna, in whose honour she wrote some splendid poems. Mirabehn ('behn' meaning 'lady') is regarded in India today as a 20th-century heroine.

In order that the reader may have a clearer background, I will explain briefly the outline of events in my life which led me to Bapu. Having been brought up in an English country home, I was familiar with rural life, besides which there was, inherent in me from the beginning, a profound love of Nature. At the age of fifteen, I first heard the music of Beethoven. Forthwith my spirit within was awakened to a living sense of the Divine Power, and prayer to God became a reality. Through Beethoven's music I became led to Romain Rolland, and through Romain Rolland to Bapu. These were not just easy stages. On the contrary turmoil, darkness, hope, despair – all had to be passed through before the pure Light of Truth

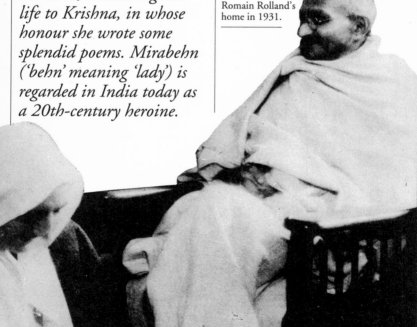

Mira and Gandhi at Romain Rolland's home in 1931.

broke in upon my troubled soul and led me to my destination.

All along a power was impelling me. I did not understand it for a long while, but, by the time I came to know of Romain Rolland, this force was becoming apparent to me, and from the time of our first meetings at Villeneuve, an extraordinary sense of mellow happiness possessed me. I felt something was coming. I had not the slightest idea *what*. I only knew that *all would be well*. Even when Romain Rolland talked to me about Bapu, and said a little book he had written about him was in the Press, I did not realize more than that I must read the book. Then the day came when the book was published. I went to the publisher's shop in the Latin Quarter of Paris, where I was then staying. The whole shop-window was full of a little book with an orange-coloured cover on which was printed in black 'Mahatma Gandhi'. I bought a copy, took it to my lodging and began to read. I could not put it down. I read and read, and as I read the dawn in my heart glowed brighter and brighter, and by the time I had finished, the Sun of Truth was pouring his rays into my soul. From that moment I knew that my life was dedicated to Bapu. That for which I had been waiting had come, and it was this.

I straightaway went to London and booked a passage to India at the P. & O. office. I also sought out and devoured all the literature I could; writings of Bapu, writings of Tagore, English and French translations of the Bhagavadgita; and even the *Upanishads* and *Vedas* I peeped into. But very soon I began to realize that I was a fool to think that I could rush to Bapu like this. I was wholly unfit spiritually and physically, and I must first put myself through a severe training. I accordingly went back to the

P. & O. office and changed my reserved berth for one a year later.

I now set about things in a thorough and systematic way. First I studied the rules and regulations of the Sabarmati Ashram in every detail. Then I began changing my diet item by item, until I reached pure vegetarian food. I started sitting cross-legged on the floor. Ten minutes at a stretch was all I could do in the beginning, but with steady practice I became perfectly at ease. I commenced lessons in Urdu and of course learnt carding, spinning and weaving. This had to be in wool, but gave me good practice. At the same time study of the literature continued. In the midst of this training news came in the papers that Bapu had gone on a twenty-one days' fast for Hindu-Muslim unity. As the days went by, the papers began saying that Bapu would probably not survive. I prayed to God in anguish. The days dragged on. But I never slackened in my training because, even if Bapu were to pass away in his physical form, I knew I must go to India to serve his cause. It seemed an eternity, but at last the twenty-one days were over and the news came that the fast had been safely broken.

Up to now I had not written a word to Bapu. But on the successful completion of the fast, my heart was so full of thankful joy that I just had to write. As a thank-offering, I enclosed in the envelope a cheque for £20. The postcard with which this book opens is Bapu's acknowledgment of that letter.

During the summer months I spent my time working with Swiss peasants in their hayfields so as to be in good trim for any physical work which might be in store for me in India. When my year's training was about three quarters over, I wrote again to Bapu reporting my

Gandhi in London (c. 1930) with Mira and the white goat that accompanied him everywhere. It provided his daily supply of milk.

progress, enclosing some samples of my yarn and asking whether I might dare to hope that I should be accepted in the Ashram. The letter which follows the first postcard is Bapu's reply. From then on my joy knew no bounds, and I lived in a state of inner ecstacy.

It might have been expected that my parents would try to dissuade me from departing, especially as my Father was closely connected with high British officials being an Admiral, and former Commander-in-Chief of the East Indies Squadron, and as my Mother and I were deeply attached to one another by

a fundamental similitude of nature. But somehow they understood the spiritual character of the urge that impelled me and never said a word to me in disapproval.

In the autumn, I paid a last visit to Villeneuve to bid farewell to Romain Rolland and his sister. Then I went back to London, packed up a few belongings and set forth. I parted with my Mother at Victoria Station and with my Father in Paris, and fate so willed it that I never saw them again.

On 25th October 1925, I boarded the P. & O. steamer at Marseilles. The voyage was one long dream of spiritual ecstacy, and the moon, as she rose night after night in the East, shed her light on the waters in a glorious silver path leading on and on towards the blessed goal.

After twelve days I landed in Bombay, and in the early morning of 7 November I reached Ahmedabad by train. Friendly faces at the station looked through the carriage window, and before I knew what had happened, I was out of the train and being seated in a car by someone who introduced himself as Vallabhbhai Patel. Another, who said he was Mahadev Desai, returned to see to the luggage. The car drove off. I looked at my companion and asked but one question – How far was the Ashram and how soon should we get there? From that day to this, everytime I see the Sardar I think of those moments of supreme suspense. We crossed the bridge over the Sabarmati river and I again asked the question. Then came fields with some houses in the distance, and I once more enquired. I was quietly told that we were still a little way off. I sat transfixed with anticipation. Suddenly my companion remarked, 'You see those trees and some buildings beyond? That is the Ashram.' In a moment the car drew up under a big tamarind tree, and I found myself walking down a little paved garden path. We passed through a small gate, then up two steps to a verandah and through a door into a room. As I entered, I became conscious of a small spare figure rising up from a white *gaddi* and stepping towards me. I knew it was Bapu, but, so completely overcome was I with reverence and joy, that I could see and feel nothing but a heavenly light. I fell on my knees at Bapu's feet. He lifted me up and taking

me in his arms said, 'You shall be my daughter.' And so has it been from that day.

I had reached my destination; the destination from which I was to begin. The old life was finished as if it belonged to a past birth, and I began life anew. And from now the real struggle began. In the old life I had groped my way through mist and fog, led by an inner urge which I could not explain. But now I emerged into the bright sunlight, and the steep, narrow Path of Truth showed clear before me leading up and up; so beautiful, and yet so hard to climb!

With boundless joy and energy, I started on the pilgrimage. Numberless times have I slipped and stumbled. Many have been the bruises and cuts. Bitter have been the tears with which I have watered the path, and once or twice the clouds have come down on the mountain and I have all but lost my way. But Bapu's love has at last led me out upon the upper pastures, where God's peace fills the sweet mountain air.

Mira
Preface to Gandhi, *Bapu's Letters to Mira (1924–48)*, 1949

Gandhi as seen by Romain Rolland

Romain Rolland was one of the first Frenchmen to take an interest in India's struggle for independence. He was fascinated by its spiritual dimension. The author of Jean-Christophe, *who received the Nobel Prize for literature in 1915, wrote biographies of the gentle Bengali mystic Ramakrishna, his disciple Vivekananda and Gandhi in 1924. In his diary he traces the development of Gandhi's ideas and personality from his early unspectacular beginnings (and mistakes) to the moment when, on his way back from the Round Table Conference in London, Gandhi, visited his famous admirer in Switzerland.*

1920

About Gandhi.

He is a lawyer from Madras [Rolland was mistaken: Gandhi came from Gujarat], who gave up all his worldly goods seven or eight years ago in order to dedicate himself to the salvation of his fellow Indians. He draws people to him like a magnet; he preaches passive resistance and discourages acts of violence.

1922

As I see him, Gandhi is anything but an internationalist in the way that I am: he is a nationalist, but a nationalist of the highest order, one who ought to serve as a model for all the petty, base or criminal nationalisms of Europe. He is an idealistic nationalist, who wants his nation to achieve spiritual supremacy – or die. And, in dominating the world by its moral greatness, he wants it to behave in a brotherly way towards the rest of the world – but as an elder brother. It is worth noting that Gandhi says that nothing would induce him to give his daughter in marriage to a Mahometan, however highly he thought of him.

1923

Gandhi as described by Andrews, a friend of Gandhi and Tagore.

According to Andrews, Gandhi is small and ordinary-looking – until he speaks – and endlessly patient. There is nothing harsh in his manner. He laughs like a child, and adores children…. At the moment he is in prison, where he is happy and asks to be left alone: he is praying and he is purifying himself, in the belief that he is doing the most useful thing he can to further India's cause.

1924

*Spiritual crisis: Gandhi and Tagore
according to Andrews.*

My dear friend, – I am staying with
Mahatma Gandhi at the moment; I have
been with him for more than a month
and a half while he has been gravely ill.
It has been a great joy and privilege
to be with him. With each passing day
I am a witness to the great beauty
of his life. There is no part of it that is
not full of sacrifice and thought for
others; he does not seem to have a single
thought for himself. There is also great
joy to be gained from observing the
life of the poet Rabindranath Tagore:
in him it is as if we see the spirit
communing with itself and finding in
solitude its own inner peace. Here, with
Mahatmaji, it is a passionate love for
others – a Christ-like love – that reigns
supreme.

I don't mean to say that Gurudev
(Tagore) leads an egoistic life: very much
the opposite. But this absence of egoism
consists in emerging from his inner
world (his permanent home) in order
to help others and deal with the trivia of
life. He told me that his happiest times
were spent living alone on a boat on the
Ganges for months on end, remaining
awake for entire nights in a state of such
profound communion with God and
Nature that he lost the need for food
or sleep. He has confided to me in our
more intimate moments how much he
misses those days now he is forced to
live in the public eye. It is a torture
for him, almost a calvary. At that time
he was a poet whose reputation was
limited to Bengal.

Mahatmaji, on the other hand, is
anxious merely to serve. Even when he
was terribly ill it was difficult to prevent
him performing some small act of

kindness that could have worn himself
out. Day and night he worried about all
the other sick people in neighbouring
beds. If the nurse seemed overworked he
wanted to look after her. And now that
he has recovered slightly and is
convalescing he has taken a couple of
sick little girls with him in order to give
them the benefit of some sea air. In such
ways he is a St Francis of Assisi. But his
intelligence is basically of a practical
kind and he uses it to address the most
complex problems of modern living.
I often used to think of him as being
'medieval' in his approach to life (and
no doubt he shows such a tendency at
times). And yet in certain respects he has
gone even further than modern science,
pondering the problems of the future in
a *scientific* fashion. In this sense he is
ultra-modern.

1928

My letter to Gandhi of 21 January
brought a lengthy response from him
dated from 14 to 17 February. Although
he is very ill, he made a point of replying
straightaway in English and of sending
the French translation of the letter (by
Mira), signed by him, at the same time.
It is evident to me that Gandhi is much
more grateful for criticism than praise
– as if he derived some exquisite secret
pleasure from it, in the same way that he
might from a refreshing and invigorating
shower. Besides he's a stubborn old
man: if you accuse him of making a
mistake, he won't give away a thing.
He loves you all the more for standing
up to him. But deep down he is a mule
– a holy mule. He neither convinces, nor
can he be convinced. He has suddenly
taken it into his head to return to
Europe and come and see me, and he is
utterly determined. I admit, it will be a
testing time and I dread it – as much for

his sake as for mine. (Even more so! Because I don't care if people think badly of me, but I don't want to think badly of someone else.)...

In short, as I understand it, Gandhi is a hero from a period of transition, torn, like so many others, between two ideals, that of the past and that of the future; over time and at some cost to himself – reluctantly, one might say – he has been obliged to give up the former. We should also bear in mind his legal training, which has encouraged him to adopt certain ways of thinking. He has always felt an instinctive respect for the State, the legal system and the army. He is not a rebel, quite the contrary.

Tagore founds the Santiniketan school

Rabindranath's grandfather was a prince and squandered his fortune, although he managed, by dubious means, to retain part of it for the benefit of his son. The son (Rabindranath's father) refused to accept the money, returning it instead to his father's creditors, who were so impressed by his honesty that they appointed him to manage his father's estate. A few years later he had succeeded, by skilful management, in paying off the debts and recovering his father's property. At fifty he abandoned everything and set off on a pilgrimage. At Santiniketan, as it is known today, beneath two trees, surrounded by a bleak and featureless plain, he had a flash of inspiration and decided to remain in the place. Rabindranath, who was then five years old, had accompanied his father and while his father prayed the young boy sang hymns. The owner of the land was so moved by the saint's piety that he gave him the land as a gift. Legend tells that while old Tagore was praying a

robber arrived with the intention of killing him, thinking that he was kneeling on some treasure; but on seeing the beauty of the old man's face as he prayed he gave up the idea and prayed with him instead. Like his father, Rabindranath is sometimes overcome by the urge to go on a religious journey. Although he loves his family and friends dearly, he disappears for months at a time, leaving home on foot or by boat. At least that was how it used to be when he was younger. Right now he is extremely tired after the recent trip he made across India in the hope of stimulating interest in his world university. The project is really taking off at the moment. No strict rules at Santiniketan, in contrast to Gandhi's Ashram, where everything is run on almost military lines: it's a military academy of asceticism!

Gandhi's first visit to Tagore, recounted by his friend William W. Pearson

Pearson describes Gandhi's first visit to Santiniketan. Tagore was not there the evening he arrived and the place was in chaos. Pearson and the other teachers offered to show him round the classrooms, but Gandhi first wanted to get an idea of the sanitary conditions and amenities of the place. He toured the building and emerged indignantly from the kitchens saying: 'The cooks are dirty. Get rid of them!' And we were obliged to dismiss them on the spot. Now that kitchen and cleaning duties had been disrupted, he put the pupils to work instead (and the teachers with them, of course). And the funny thing was that from the word go everyone did what he said. We were no longer in charge, says Pearson, and the pupils all carried out his orders with great

Gandhi visits the writer Romain Rolland at his home in Villeneuve, Switzerland, in 1931.

enthusiasm. 'What kind of voice does he have?' I ask, and Pearson replies: 'He hasn't got a voice. In public he speaks no louder than we are now' (sitting on different sides of the same table). 'Then no one can hear him?' 'No one can hear him. But the crowd all watch his lips and follow him blindly. He's extraordinarily charismatic.' As for influencing his decisions, forget it. You can talk and talk, but it won't change a thing. When he was in the Transvaal, Gokhal, for whom he had the greatest respect, and who was on the point of death and might pass away at any moment, sent him daily telegrams begging him to sign an act that Gandhi had no wish to sign. Gandhi knew that by refusing he could be hastening Gokhal's death, but nothing could make him change his mind.

1932

The 'epic fast', as described by Gandhi to Romain Rolland.

What I want, what I live for, and would be happy to die for, is the eradication of Untouchability. I want a living pact whose rejuvenating effects will be felt today, right now, and not in some distant future; and this pact must be sealed by a demonstration throughout India, with Touchables and Untouchables coming together and embracing one another as brothers.... My life has no importance. I believe that if they sacrificed a hundred lives in this noble cause Hindus would be doing pathetically little to expiate all the horrific injustices they have heaped on defenceless men and women.... If I had anything more to give I would set this too in the balance as a way of removing the stigma. But all I have is my life....

I believe that if Untouchability is genuinely rooted out not only will Hinduism be cleansed of a terrible stain, but the repercussions of such an action will be felt worldwide. My struggle against Untouchability is a struggle against all that is impure in humanity. For this reason I am fully convinced that the best people in this great family of men will support me....

Romain Rolland
Inde, journal, 1915–43, 1951

Alexandra David-Neel on the subject of Gandhi's death

She was known as the 'woman with the winged feet', an indefatigable mystic who spent weeks tramping across the Himalayas. Unfailingly perceptive about India's contradictions, Alexandra David-Neel describes the true reasons for Gandhi's assassination, vehemently denouncing the dangers — still evident today — of 'ultra-orthodox' Hinduism.

A lexandra David-Neel in 1948, the year this article was published.

Since the proclamation of India's independence, anyone interested in the politics of Asia could not fail to have noticed the conflicts between Pakistan and Hindu India and the resulting massacres. And yet the enmity that exists between Muslims and Hindus is not the only problem in India; there is a further problem of no less significance for national peace: ultra-orthodox Hinduism.

(In what follows I shall use the term 'Indian' to indicate … a native of India. The name 'Hindu' applies, more precisely, to those who profess Hinduism, Hinduism being a religious denomination.)

For a long time it seemed as if the sole aim of the Indian people was to induce the British to quit India, but this was not in fact the case. Indians have never regarded the departure of the British as anything more than a precondition, one that was indispensable if they were to succeed in their true aims. I say *aims*, in the plural, because there are many of them, each corresponding to the different and sometimes contradictory ideals of the various sections of the population.

In India I have seen crowds of Muslim demonstrators shouting 'Pakistan! Pakistan!', while an educated Brahman said to me: 'We'll sacrifice Gandhi to Kali.'

And the prophecies came true. Pakistan exists as an independent state and Gandhi has been assassinated … sacrificed to Kali.

Philosophers see Kali as one of the ten symbolic forms of universal energy, or Shakti, but for the bulk of her followers Kali is a black-faced goddess adorned with a necklace of human heads. She was the special protector of the Thugs, those sinister mystics who worshipped her by strangling their human victims in her name. For the Brahman who had talked of sacrificing Gandhi to her, Kali represented Hindu ultra-orthodoxy.

Western newspapers described in detail the demonstrations that followed Gandhi's death, and the sight of millions of Hindus in mourning fostered the impression in the West that Gandhi personified the workings of India in all its aspects. This was in fact very far from the truth.

India's vast population can be measured in millions. And though it is certainly true that many mourned the 'Mahatma', many others – perhaps more – regarded him as a renegade and the enemy of Hinduism.

Who are these ultra-orthodox Hindus – members of the 'Grand Society', the Mahasabha, and other associations with similar tendencies? They are reactionaries convinced of their own superiority in religious and social matters.

We need not concern ourselves with their aims. These people are motivated by a national pride that is stronger than anything ever witnessed in Nazi Germany. In their eyes anyone not born a Hindu is a barbarian, unclean, a *mletcha* unworthy of attention. The one thing that Western countries have to fear on their account is that they might gain political ascendancy in India and so deepen the gulf which already exists between East and West.

What is it that these ultra-orthodox Hindus want?... Quite simply they would like to reintroduce in India the kind of society that prevailed several centuries ago, while the more fanatical among them go still further by seeking to establish a society that has only ever existed in Hindu legend and mythology.

In my talks with Gandhi it became clear to me that he was not nearly as progressive as he was thought to be outside India; and yet, though this lawyer and ex-student of the University of London was not very 'modern' in his outlook, orthodox Hindus found him too lukewarm in his admiration for that distant past which so fascinated them and questioned his belief in the possible revival of that 'golden age'.

Orthodox worship is quite distinctive, involving rites and sacrifices. Worshippers cut the throats of goats in honour of Kali and in some places – Nepal for example – shed the blood of buffaloes, but Kali used to smile on nobler victims and her followers believe she still has an appetite for them. 'The Mother (Kali) wants human victims, but the British will not let us give her any,' I was told one day by a worshipper as I approached one of the goddess's altars.

Those who took a rigid orthodox line regarded Gandhi as neither a saint, nor a sage, but as a 'politician', readily contrasting him with one of their compatriots, Shri Aurobindo, whom they saw as embodying the ancient ideal of wisdom. Shri Aurobindo, 'the greatest man in India', was a learned philosopher who had involved himself in politics in his youth and long since repented the error of his ways. He led an extraordinarily cloistered life at his home in Pondicherry, surrounded by a group of zealous disciples who credited him with supra-divine status.

The supporters of Hindu orthodoxy show little enthusiasm for Gandhi's policy of non-violence. Indeed, it goes against the express commandment of the divine Krishna, avatar of Vishnu, as he expresses it in the most widely read of all the Hindu religious texts, the Bhagavadgita.

A woman about to commit suttee, one of the Hindu 'barbaric practices' criticized by Alexandra David-Neel.

There is a scene in the poem where Arjuna, prince of the warrior caste, is hesitating on the eve of battle, his heart full of pity for his enemy. 'What joy will there be for us in killing these people?' he asks. 'How could we be happy afterwards....'

While he is thinking these thoughts the prince drops his bow, 'for his heart was fluttering with pain.'.

Krishna appears, however, and reproaches him vehemently for his hesitation: 'Fight against weakness.... Be done with childish cowardice. Get up! Fight! There is nothing better than a battle in a just cause.... If you abandon your duty every living creature will broadcast your shame, and shame is worse than death.... Fight, therefore, son of India.'

'Fight!', 'Strike!', says Krishna, and Gandhi, who pleaded against attacking one's enemy, or even defending oneself against an aggressor, had at times in the course of his struggles seemed like a renegade to the supporters of the old revolutionary orthodoxy.

They reproached him for having, on several occasions, 'taken sides' with the British. That Gandhi's lack of intransigence might be explained in terms of political acumen is something that the ultra-orthodox have never been able, nor sought, to understand. I remember the fury of a young student who described to me how, during a

period of patriotic fervour, he and some of his friends had engaged in acts of dangerous sabotage – on Gandhi's instructions, he said – only to learn that the 'Mahatma' disavowed revolutionary activity.

In this as in similar cases there may have been misunderstandings, but it is quite clear that the fanatic who foresaw Gandhi's death as a sacrifice to Kali, that other fanatic who failed to assassinate the 'Mahatma' and the one who succeeded were not rare exceptions. Many Hindus had already mentally passed sentence on Gandhi and some among them may be now directing their thoughts towards other victims.

Despite their frequently harsh attitude towards Indians, the British have lacked the courage to root out the superstitions and barbaric practices fostered by popular Hinduism. A few of these have disappeared, but the beliefs upon which they were based remain as vigorous as ever. Now that the British yoke has been lifted, will the reactionaries not attempt to restore all those ancient traditions which were either prohibited or obstructed under British rule, in particular the marriage of girls of eight or nine to men of thirty or forty, or older?

Horrifying though this latter practice is, we should not be in a hurry to declare it infeasible in our day and age. I myself have known two cases. In both it was said that the victim made the sacrifice of her own free will. The British legal establishment nevertheless condemned those who had collaborated in the torture of the two unfortunate young girls…. Today, however, the British are no longer there….

We should rightly have confidence in the progressive elements of the Indian population – men and women of remarkable intelligence, capable of drawing excellent practical lessons from the lofty philosophical notions that have come down to them from the past. But will they be allowed the freedom to exercise such abilities?… Will they still dare to stand up to the reactionaries, when those reactionaries with their disastrous ideas are capable of arming the fanatics against them?… The risk is great; Gandhi's tragic death proves it.

Alexandra David-Neel
Journal de Genève, 9 March 1948

Gandhi psychoanalysed

In the wake of Gandhi's death numerous biographies appeared, many of them written – with exacting attention to detail – by his most loyal disciples. The more impartial accounts that followed, while not seeking to detract from his achievements, considered the great hero of independence in a more objective light. Sudhir Kakar is a psychoanalyst – one of the few to have come out of India – who studied under Erik Erikson, himself the author of a book on the Mahatma, and the following is taken from Kakar's study of Indian sexuality.

Some of Gandhi's uneasiness with phallic desire has to do with his feeling that genital love is an accursed and distasteful prerogative of the father. In his autobiography, in spite of expressing many admirable filial sentiments, Gandhi suspects his father of being 'oversexed' since he married for the fourth time when he was over forty and Putlibai, Gandhi's mother, was only eighteen. In his fantasy, we would suggest, Gandhi saw his young mother as the innocent victim of a powerful old male's lust to which the child could only be an anguished and helpless spectator, unable to save the beloved caretaker from the violation of her person and the violence done to her body. In later life, Gandhi would embrace the cause wherein the marriage of old men with young girls was adamantly opposed with great zeal. He wrote articles with such titles as 'Marriage of Old and Young or Debauchery?' and exhorted his correspondents who reported such incidents to fight this practice. The older men he respected and took as his models were those who shared his revulsion with genital sexuality. These were the men who (like Tolstoy and Raichandra) had sought to transform sexual passion into a more universal religious quest or (like Ruskin) into a moral and aesthetic fervor.

If phallic desire was the violent and tumultuous 'way of the fathers', genital abstinence, its surrender, provided the tranquil, peaceful path back to the mother. Here Gandhi was not unlike St Augustine, who too inwardly beheld celibacy garbed in soothing, maternal imagery: 'There appeared unto me the chaste dignity of Continence, serene, yet not relaxedly gay, honestly alluring me to come and doubt not; and stretching forth to receive and embrace me, her

Kasturbai and Gandhi.

holy hands full of multitudes of good examples; there were so many young men and maidens here, a multitude of youth and every age, grave widows and aged virgins; and Continence herself in all, not barren, but a fruitful mother of children of joys.'

More specifically, the psycho-biographical evidence we have reviewed above is compelling that Gandhi's relationships with women are dominated by the unconscious fantasy of maintaining an idealized relationship with the maternal body. This wished-for oneness with the mother is suffused with nurturance and gratitude, mutual adoration and affirmation, without a trace of desire which divides and bifurcates. Replete with wishes for fusion and elimination of differences and limits, Gandhi 'perceived' sexual desire, *both* of the mother and the child, as the single biggest obstacle to the

preservation of this illusion. Many of his attitudes, beliefs and actions with regard to women can then be understood as defensive maneuvers against the possibility of this perception rising to surface awareness.

Since the mother is a woman, a first step in the defensive operations is to believe that women are not, or only minimally, sexual beings. 'I do not believe that woman is prey to sexual desire to the same extent as man. It is easier for her than for man to exercise self-restraint,' is an opinion often repeated in his writings. Reflecting on his own experiences with Kasturbai, he asserts that 'There was never want of restraint on the part of my wife. Very often she would show restraint, but she rarely resisted me, although she showed disinclination very often.' Whereas he associates male sexuality with unheeding, lustful violence, female sexuality, where it exists, is a passive, suffering acceptance of the male onslaught. This, we must again remember, is only at the conscious level. Unconsciously, his perception of masculine violence and feminine passivity seem [sic] to be reversed, as evident in the imagery of the descriptions of his few erotic encounters with women. In his very first adolescent confrontation, he is struck 'dumb and blind', while the woman is confident and aggressive; in England, he is trembling like a frightened wild animal who has just escaped the (woman) hunter.

The solution to the root problem between the sexes is, then, not a removal of the social and legal inequalities suffered by women – though Gandhi was an enthusiastic champion of women's rights – but a thoroughgoing desexualization of the male-female relationship, in which women must take the lead. 'If they will only learn to say "no" to their husbands when they approach them carnally.... If a wife says to her husband: "No, I do not want it," he will make no trouble. But she has not been taught.... I want women to learn the primary right of resistance.'

Besides desexing the woman, another step in the denial of her desire is her idealization (especially of the Indian woman) as nearer to a purer divine state and thus an object of worship and adoration. That is why a woman does not need to renounce the world in the last stage of life to contemplate God, as is prescribed for the man in the ideal Hindu life cycle. 'She sees Him always. She has no need of any other school to prepare her for Heaven than marriage to a man and care of her children.' Woman is also 'the incarnation of *Ahimsa, Ahimsa* means infinite love, which, again, means infinite capacity for suffering. Who but woman, the mother of man, shows this capacity in the largest measure? Let her transfer that love to the whole of humanity, let her forget she ever was, or can be, the object of man's lust. And she will occupy her proud position by the side of the man as his mother, maker and silent leader.'

Primarily seeing the mother in the woman and idealizing motherhood is yet another way of denying feminine eroticism. When Millie Polak, a female associate in the Phoenix *ashram* in South Africa, questioned his idealization of motherhood, saying that being a mother does not make a woman wise, Gandhi extolled mother-love as one of the finest aspects of love in human life. His imagery of motherhood is of infants suckling on breasts with inexhaustible supplies of milk. For example, in a letter explaining why the Gita, the sacred

book of the Hindus, is called Mother, he rhapsodizes, 'It has been likened to the sacred cow, the giver of all desires (sic!). Hence Mother. Well, that immortal Mother gives all the milk we need for spiritual sustenance, if we would but approach her as babies seeking and sucking it from her. She is capable of yielding milk to her millions of babies from her exhaustless udder.... '

Whereas desexualizing, idealizing and perceiving only the 'milky' mother in the woman is one part of his defensive bulwark which helped in preserving the illusion of unity with the maternal body intact, the other part consists of efforts at renouncing the gift of sexual desire, abjuring his own masculinity. Here we must note that the Hindu Vaishnava culture, in which Gandhi grew up and in which he remained deeply rooted, not only provides a sanction for man's feminine strivings, but raises these strivings to the level of a religious-spiritual quest. In devotional Vaishnavism, Lord Krishna alone is the male and all devotees, irrespective of their sex, are female. Gandhi's statement that he had mentally become a woman or that he envied women and that there is as much reason for a man to wish that he was born a woman, as for women to do otherwise, thus struck many responsive chords in his audience.

If Gandhi had had his way, there would be no art or poetry celebrating woman's beauty. 'I am told that our literature is full of even an exaggerated apotheosis of women. Let me say that it is an altogether wrong apotheosis. Let me place one simple fact before you. In what light do you think of them when you proceed to write about them? I suggest that before you put your pens to paper [you] think of women as your own mother, and I assure you the

Gandhi 'adores children' (Romain Rolland).

chastest literature will flow from your pens, even like the beautiful rain from heaven which waters the thirsty earth below. Remember that a woman was your mother, before a woman became your wife.'

Although Gandhi's wished-for feminization was defensive in origin, we cannot deny the development of its adaptive aspects. Others, most notably Erik Erikson, have commented upon Gandhi's more or less conscious explorations of the maternal stance and feminine perspective in his actions. In spite of a welter of public demands on his time, we know of the motherly care he could extend to the personal lives of his followers, and the anxious concern he displayed about their health and well-being, including solicitous enquiries about the state of their daily bowel movements. We also know of the widening of these maternal-feminine ways – teasing, testing, taking suffering upon oneself, and so on – in the formulation of his political style and as elements of his campaigns of militant non-violence.

Sudhir Kakar
Intimate Relations:
Exploring Indian Sexuality, 1990

GLOSSARY

ahimsa Non-violence, a key concept of Jainism, which developed in India at the same time as Buddhism and profoundly influenced the Mahatma, in whose native Gujarat it is widely practised. Followers of this austere religion are bound by a number of vows (*vrata*): not to harm any living creature; to avoid falsehood and lies; not to steal; to curb sexual desires; and to relinquish all attachment to worldly goods. *Ahimsa* is the first of the *vrata* and devotees of Jainism go to great lengths to honour this vow: Jains may often be seen carefully sweeping the path in front of them with a small brush to avoid trampling on an insect, and they wear a small piece of white cloth over their mouths to avoid swallowing an insect by mistake. Jainism is rigidly structured and its followers are required to pass through fourteen stages before attaining spiritual peace, being free at the twelfth stage to starve themselves to death and so quit their physical body. Today there are an estimated two million Jains in India.

ashram Originally an ashram was a natural refuge – the top of a mountain, a cave, forest or glacier – to which a holy man would retire for the purpose of meditation or penance. The term was then extended to include monasteries, hermitages and communities founded by gurus or spiritual leaders. The *ashramas* are also the four stages in the life of a Brahman: *brahmacharya*, the life of the student; *garhasthya*, life in the world as a family man; *vanaprasthya*, retreat from the world, asceticism and detachment; and finally *samnyasa*, the life of total aceticism, sometimes wandering, but always solitary. Gandhi did not actively distinguish between the four life stages of the Brahmans (a caste to which he did not belong), merely appropriating from them a set of moral rules.

banyan (*Ficus benghalensis*) A tree whose aerial roots grow down into the soil to form additional trunks. The banyan, which is dedicated to the creator god Vishnu, can grow to an immense size and often serves as a focal point for meetings or prayers at the centre of Indian villages.

Brahman Hindu society is traditionally divided into four major hereditary castes which confer social rank, determine a person's profession and establish watertight religious boundaries between persons of different caste. At the head of this system is the literate priestly caste of Brahmans, the privileged keepers of religious knowledge who alone may recite the scriptures and perform sacrifices or *pujas*. Born, according to legend, from the head of Brahma, the great creator god, Brahmans are 'twice born': once from their mother's womb, and a second time during adolescence when they don the sacred sash, a sign of their learning and high status. Traditionally Brahmans were barred from secular work, but in India today they have carved an important niche for themselves in the professions. It is important to remember that Gandhi, unlike Nehru, was not a Brahman.

brahmacharya The Brahman, like the Jain, follows a spiritual path that begins in adolescence and involves a series of stages and vows. The vow of chastity, or *brahmacharya*, is an inseparable part of this education and of life in the ashram.

Brahmo Samaj Reform movement founded by Rammohan Ray (1772–1833), a linguist born in Bengal who specialized in English, Persian, Arabic and Sanskrit. He was one of the first Hindus to criticize the caste system and the practices of polygamy and suttee (self-immolation on a husband's funeral pyre) – the latter being abolished, thanks to him, in 1829. He campaigned in favour of women's education and the opportunity for widows to remarry, and his modernizing ideas earned him the title the 'Father of modern India'. He was sent to London to represent the emperor Akbar III and died in Bristol.

darshan Sanskrit word signifying, among other things, a demonstration, a vision, or a philosophy. In its most commonly used religious sense the *darshan* or 'vision' of a saint or statue (or of a political leader) is supposed to transfer to the spectator some of the properties of the object of worship:

the object 'offers' or 'gives up' its *darshan* to the worshippers as they feast upon it with their eyes. Gandhi disliked the notion of *darshan* but could not avoid fuelling it by his public appearances.

dharma The general law of the universe, in relation to which the term 'individual' loses all meaning, each living creature being an integral part of the cosmic order. *Karma* denotes the sum of all human actions, which is passed from one individual existence to the next and determines the nature of the individual's rebirth within the world *dharma*.

Dravidians A number of aboriginal races living in southern India who use different languages from the Indo-Europeans. The great popular epic the Ramayana mythologizes the age-old conflict between Aryans and Dravidians. It tells the story of a northern king, Rama, a model of divine perfection, whose wife is abducted by a demon-god from the south; Rama goes to reclaim her, devastating the southern kingdoms in the process. The political tension mythologized in the Ramayana subsists in certain areas of India, in particular Tamil Nadu, where the cause of Dravidian nationalism has found a powerful voice in the Dravida Munnetra Kazhagam party.

fakir A Muslim mendicant who practises religious and ascetic exercises. In India the term is applied to any (Muslim or Hindu) ascetic or yogi.

hartal Silent protest demonstration during which prayers are said and all social activity is suspended. What distinguishes a *hartal* from a national strike is the complete lack of non-violence and the fact that it is not aimed at winning political advantage.

khadi The movement to promote the indigenous manufacture of cotton by rejecting excessively priced Indian cotton imported from Britain. Gradually it came to include all handmade goods and *khadi* shops sold all the traditional items of clothing worn by the *swadeshi*.

Kshatriyas The caste of warriors and kings, caretakers of world order. Although a king

(rajah or maharajah) might be immensely wealthy and Brahmans often come from very poor families, the Kshatryia caste is nevertheless inferior to the priestly Brahman caste. Georges Dumézil was the first to note that, among the Indo-European races, the first three castes corresponded to the principal powers in ancient Rome and fulfilled the same primary social functions.

sadhu A holy man who has reached the fourth stage in the life of a Brahman, having renounced all worldly goods. Sadhus lead a wandering life and are dependent on alms. They are distinctive figures, often naked, with painted bodies and long, matted hair ritually covered with ash, carrying nothing but a stick, a brass pot (*lotta*) and a bag in their hand.

Shudra The fourth caste in the Hindu system, to which the manual workers and labourers belong.

Untouchable In the Hindu caste system the lowest level of society, the damned souls condemned to live the life of human vultures.

Vaishya It was to the Vaishyas, the third caste in the Hindu system, that Gandhi himself belonged. Their role relates to the earth and Vaishyas traditionally make their living from agriculture, stock rearing and the skilled manufacture of goods. Thought to have been born from Brahma's thigh, they are nevertheless barred from book learning and unable to attain spiritual deliverance.

yoga A body of philosophical doctrines designed to lead to a state of release and liberation from the material world through physical control and meditative (in particular breathing) techniques. The yoga practitioner is known as a yogi.

yogi Like the Jains yogis must respect all forms of life and follow the path of truth, cleanliness, chastity, asceticism, morality and spiritual enlightenment. The extraordinary physical feats achieved by yogis – the way, for example, they can be buried alive and yet survive – have been a source of fascination to Western scientists for two hundred years.

FURTHER READING

Azad, Maulana Abdul Kalam, *India Wins Freedom*, 1960

Bhagavadgita, translated by Swami Vireswaranda, 1983

Bapu's Letters to Mira (1924–48), 1949

Besant, Annie, *The Case for India*, 1918

——, *The Future of Indian Politics*, 1922

——, *How India Wrought for Freedom: The Story of the National Congress, told from Official Records*, 1915

Bhattacharya, Sachchidananda, *A Dictionary of Indian History*, 1967

Boisselier, Jean, *The Wisdom of the Buddha*, 1994

David-Neel, Alexandra, *Buddhism: Its Methods and Its Doctrines*, translated by H. N. M. Hardy and Bernard Miall, 1939

——, *L'Inde où j'ai vécu: Avant et après l'indépendance*, 1951

Erikson, Erik H., *Gandhi's Truth*, 1969

Fischer, Louis, *The Essential Gandhi*, 1962

——, *Gandhi and Stalin*, 1947

——, *The Life of Mahatma Gandhi*, 1951

——, *A Week with Gandhi*, 1942

Gandhi, Mahatma, *Bapu's Letters to Mira*, 1949

——, *The Collected Works*, 90 vols., 1919–58

——, *Gandhiji's Fifth Fast*, 1943

——, *Hind Swaraj or Indian Home Rule*, 1938

——, *Indian Opinion*, 1904–14

——, *My Early Life*, 1932

——, *Satyagraha in South Africa*, 1928

——, *Speeches and Writings*, 1933

——, *The Story of My Experiments with Truth*, translated by Mahadev Desai, 1927–9

——, *Young India 1919–22*, 1924

——, *Young India 1924–6*, 1927

Gandhi, Manubehn, *The End of an Epoch*, translated by Gopalkrishna Gandhi, 1962

——, *Last Glimpses of Bapu*, translated by Moti Lal Jain, 1962

Gandhi, Rajmohan, *The Good Boatman: A Portrait of Gandhi*, 1995

Kakar, Sudhir, *Intimate Relations: Exploring Indian Sexuality*, 1990

Kripalani, Krishna, *Gandhi, A Life*, 1968

Nehru, Jawaharlal, *An Autobiography*, 1936

——, *The Discovery of India*, 1946

——, *Mahatma Gandhi*, 1949

The Penguin Gandhi Reader, ed. R. Mukherjo, 1993

Patel, Sushil Kumar, *Hinduism in India: A Study of Vishnu Worship*, 1992

Pyarelal, *The Epic Fast*, 1932

Rolland, Romain, *Essai sur la mystique et l'action de l'Inde vivante*, 1960

——, *Inde, journal, 1915–43*, 1951

——, *The Life of Ramakrishna*, translated by E. F. Malcolm-Smith, 1965

——, *Mahatma Gandhi: The Man who Became One with the Universal Being*, translated by Catherine D. Groth, 1924

Shearer, Alistair, *Buddha: The Intelligent Heart*, 1992

——, *The Hindu Vision: Forms of the Formless*, 1993

Smith, Vincent A., *The Oxford History of India*, 1985

Tendulkar, D. G., *Mahatma: Life of Mohandas Karamchand Gandhi*, 8 vols., 1951–4

Thomas, K. P., *Kasturba Gandhi: A Biographical Study*, 1944

FILMOGRAPHY

Aparajito (also called *The Unvanquished*), written and directed by Satyajit Ray, 1956

Calcutta, directed by Louis Malle, 1969

The Chess Players, written and directed by Satyajit Ray, 1977

Gandhi, directed by Richard Attenborough, 1982

Heat and Dust, directed by James Ivory, 1982

Lives of a Bengal Dancer, directed by Henry Hathaway, 1935

The Music Room, written and directed by Satyajit Ray, 1958

Passage to India, written and directed by David Lean, 1984

Pather Panchali, written and directed by Satyajit Ray, 1955

Phantom India, directed by Louis Malle, 1969

The Rains Came, directed by Clarence Brown, 1939

The River, directed by Jean Renoir, 1951

Salaam Bombay!, directed by Mira Nair, 1988

The World of Apu, written and directed by Satyajit Ray, 1959

LIST OF ILLUSTRATIONS

CHAPTER 2

CHAPTER 3

DOCUMENTS

INDEX

ACKNOWLEDGMENTS

The author wishes in particular to thank the staff at the Nehru Memorial Library, her friends J. C. Kapur, Sudhir Kakar, and most especially Mrs Pupul Jayakar; also Hélène Cixous, Ariane Mnouchkine, Philippe Lenglet, Pierre Amado, François Gros and Francis Warcziarg.

The publishers would like to thank the following individuals and organizations for helping to make the publication of this book possible: the staff at the National Gandhi Museum in Delhi; Miss Houssein and Mr Chanda Tirthankar of the Indian Embassy in Paris; the photographer Romain Warcziarg; Martine Huvelin; Pascal Bonafoux; and Patrick Mérienne for the map.

PHOTO CREDITS

All rights reserved spine, 1–9, 12, 13, 14, 16a, 16b, 17, 18, 18–9, 20al, 20ar, 20bl, 20br, 21, 22a, 22b, 23al, 23b, 28l, 30b, 32, 40–1, 42, 43, 54, 56–7, 59r, 63l, 65, 70–1, 86, 92r, 94–5a, 94–5b, 96–7a, 100–1a, 100–1b, 104, 109r, 115r, 140, 141, 143. Paul Almasy, Thoiry 105. BBC Hulton Picture Library, London 46, 55r. Bibliothèque Nationale, Paris 42–3, 160–1. Bridgeman, London 30a. J.-L. Charmet, Paris 26–7, 36, 44, 53r, 82–3. Collection Sirot-Angel, Paris 34, 40, 102, 103, 152. Dagli-Orti, Paris 84, 85. Edimedia, Paris 26, 93, 127. Enguerand, Paris 163, 165, 172. Government of India Information Services, New York front cover. Illustrated London News Picture Library, London 60. Indian Embassy, Service Information, Paris 31, 55l, 72, 75, 88, 92l, 142, 157. Keystone, Paris 51, 63r, 68, 69, 74b, 78a, 80c, 80b, 80–1, 87a, 87b, 94, 96–7b, 107, 108, 114–5, 120–1a, 149. Magnum/Henri Cartier-Bresson 111a, 116–7, 118–9, 120, 120–1b, 144. Musée de l'Homme, Paris 134. National Gandhi Museum, Delhi 11, 28r, 38, 39l, 39r, 45l, 45r, 48–9, 49, 50, 53l, 62–3, 64, 66b, 66–7, 74a, 76–7, 80a, 89, 98, 99, 110–1, 113, 122l, 124a, 124–5, 125a, 128, 129, 130, 136, 145, 146, 147. National Portrait Gallery, London 14–5. Jean-Louis Nou, Paris 23ar, 24ar, 24bl, 24br. Popperfoto, London 78–9, 106, 112. Rapho/Roland and Sabrina Michaud back cover, 24al, 25a, 25b, 29, 34–5. Roger-Viollet, Paris 15r, 37, 53c, 58–9, 66a, 78b, 91, 126, 133, 150, 158. Roger-Viollet/Harlingue, Paris 47, 60–1. Roger-Viollet/Lapi 90. VIP/Sipa Icono 122–3.

TEXT CREDITS

Grateful acknowledgment is made for use of material from the following works: (pp. 34, *44*, *49*, 61–2, 79–80, 91, 93, 98, *99*, *121*, 127, 146–7) Louis Fischer, *The Life of Mahatma Gandhi*, Jonathan Cape, 1951; reprinted with permission of Random House UK Ltd, London, and George Uri Fischer. (pp. 150–3) Gandhi, *Bapu's Letter to Mira (1924–48)*, Navajivan Publishing House, 1949; reprinted with permission of the Navajivan Trust, Ahmedabad, India. (pp. 30, 32, *32*, 39, 41, *41*, 55, 130–5, 136–41, 142–3, 148–9) Gandhi, *The Collected Works of Mahatma Gandhi*, Navajivan Publishing House, 1919–58; reprinted with permission of the Navajivan Trust, Ahmedabad, India. (pp. 162–5) Sudhir Kakar, *Intimate Relations: Exploring Indian Sexuality*, University of Chicago Press, 1990; copyright © Sudhir Kakar 1989; the quotation on pp. 162–5 is reproduced courtesy the publishers (Penguin Books India Pvt. Ltd and the University of Chicago Press) and the author.

Catherine Clément
is a writer and philosopher. She has published
sixteen essays (including *Les Fils de Freud sont fatigués,
Vies et légendes de Jacques Lacan, L'Opéra ou la défaite des
femmes, Lévi-Strauss ou la structure et le malheur* and
Le Goût du miel) and nine novels (including *Edwina
and Nehru: A Romance, La Sultane*
and *Bleu Panique*).

For Randhir Singh

Translated from the French by Ruth Sharman

Series manager, Harry N. Abrams, Inc.: Eve Sinaiko

Library of Congress Catalog Card Number: 96–83342

ISBN 0–8109–2803–5

Published in 1996 by Harry N. Abrams, Inc., New York
A Times Mirror Company

Printed and bound in Italy by Editoriale Libraria, Trieste